BECOMING AN ADVERTISING CREATIVE: MADE TERRIFYING

by
Andy Beach

Written with great gratitude to all my students, past, present and future, even though one day you'll be stealing my job.

And thanks to my lovely wife, Jessica, who read and helped edit this book, even though the content was of zero interest to her.

PART I:
SOME PREP WORK

INTRODUCTION

*H*i. I'm Andy. Thanks for buying this book, or borrowing it, or stealing it. I hope you've done the former as opposed to the latter because stealing, especially from me, is wrong. But regardless, it's nice to have you along and I hope you finish this book feeling fully informed and having had a few smiles along the way. I'll note that you should also consider reading this book to have been worthwhile if you end up deciding you want no part of this whole ad creative thing. This book is not a sales pitch. It's what I feel to be an accurate guide to what's involved in getting a gig as an ad creative. It also includes some hints on what it's like working in the business. I'm sure my bias (I personally love the biz) will come out here and there, but I'll do my best to keep things right down the middle. You'll find that I'm a big supporter of actually enjoying your work. So, if from reading this book you come to the conclusion that you'll enjoy NOT working in advertising, then I'd say the following words have done their job.

Also, given the fact that I'm an experienced instructor of aspiring ad creatives, expect some sage advice and mental preparation. I'd like to leave you not only informed, but also as emotionally prepared as possible. I say, "as possible," because there ain't no way a book is going to fully prepare you for the journey ahead should you decide you want to become an ad creative. It's my hope that this mental preparation will also be helpful in guiding you to your decision.

Either way, "Yes, please" or "No thanks," I hope you like my book and are glad you picked it up.

WHY SHOULD I LISTEN TO YOU ANYWAY, ANDY BEACH?

Good question. And a fair one, so I'll do my best to answer (even though I've already got your money). First, for you who-the-hell-is-this-guy-and-what-has-he-done types, I'll give a bit of professional background. This will come in the form of a brief history of Andy Beach, which will reveal how I got to the point that I've decided I'm qualified to write a book. Then, I'll give an emotional, spiritual, ponytail guy (even though I don't have a ponytail. Actually I don't have much hair at all) answer to why I felt compelled to write a book. I think this answer is just as important as my professional background. The thing is, anyone can do research and slap together a book on the steps you need to take to get into advertising. But, my dear friends, only a loving, gentle soul, such as myself, will put real concern and enthusiasm, and all that Pollyanna stuff into my advice (Google "Pollyanna," if you're young and don't know what the hell I'm talking about). First, a bit about my background and how I got to the point where I think I'm qualified to sell you my advice.

I knew from pretty early on that being an ad creative was how I wanted to make my living. I discovered around junior high or so that I was a pretty gifted writer (after reading this book, you may or may not agree). Obviously I wasn't agonizing over career choices in seventh grade, but I started to think that a career in writing could be in the cards for me. Over time, however, I began to see that I didn't really have they type of attention span that made me believe I could be a novelist (this book sure as hell took long enough to write), so I was still in the dark about exact career plans. But I still had time to figure it out.

Then towards the end of high school when I actually needed to start making some decisions about a college major, I suddenly thought, "Hey, some-one comes up with commercials. Why not me?" So I started pursuing a career in advertising.

After a bit of JuCo (that's junior college for those of you Ivy Leagu-ers) time at Sierra College, I went to San Jose State, and graduated with a BS in Advertising in '98.

So then I got a job as an ad creative, right? Wrong.

Much love and respect to SJSU's staff, but the ad program at SJSU didn't give me what I really needed to get a job as a creative. The fact is, most universities just aren't set up to give students who want to be creatives everything they need to get a job. What I mean by this will become more clear as you read on. But I was determined. I was armed with a diploma, but unfortunately not much else I needed to become an ad creative. Though I was bummed, for me there was no second option for a career path, so I did what I had to do.
So long story short, after graduation I worked hard, on my own, for two years. With some great advice from professional contacts that worked in the ad business, I finally built what I needed: a good student portfolio (more information on what a student portfolio is later). In January, 2000, I got my shot as a Junior Copywriter at J. Walter Thompson in San Jose, California. Hoooray!

Soon after I got hired, being one of the few San Jose State Alums to get a job as an ad creative, I started to get contacted by the SJSU ad club to come speak. So I did, and I liked it. A lot. I seemed to have a knack for it, so I got invited back to speak some more. Professors also started inviting me to speak to their classes. They all thought this Andy Beach was a good guy who had something to offer students. I was really glad about that, because it was a lot of fun. It also felt great to have the opportunity to help San Jose State students and tell them what was really up when it comes to getting a job as a creative. But I wasn't done with this helping students thing. Not by a long shot.

A few years into my career at JWT, four lovely young interns showed up in the offices of JWT. They were all from the advertising grad program at The Academy of Art University in San Francisco. One day, I was chatting with a couple of them as I liked to do (they were really cool, very funny and, you know, girls), and they happened to mention that most of their instructors at the Academy were working ad creatives. I thought to myself, "Hey, I'm a working ad creative and I have this knack for helping out students. I should teach!" So I got myself a job teaching in the Academy of Art University's graduate advertising program and started instructing aspiring advertising creatives.

I've been at it for while now. I've also taught at Miami Ad School's San Francisco campus. I've even gone as far as set up my own little school a few times in a rented classroom, recruiting students from San Jose State. I've got a pretty good handle on both the ad business and getting into the ad business, so I figured I could write a pretty good book about it.

So here's the spiritual hippy answer on why you should listen to me. It's much shorter: I deeply and sincerely care about ad creative students.

After well over half a decade of helping students through one of the most difficult, emotionally draining plights of their young lives (or maybe a little bit older lives, for the second career types), it's become a very important part of my life. I love hearing about former students getting their first jobs (actually, I've been at it long enough I'm hearing about former students getting their second and third jobs). I love seeing them bounce back from a rough stretch when they're not coming up with anything they can be proud of. I love when people hunting for their first job get a hold of my email address somehow and contact me for help. From the moment I felt I had something to offer people looking to get into this business, I've gladly given whatever time I had to help out.

I've never forgotten how much it meant to me when I got to meet real live advertising creatives working in honest-to-goodness ad agencies, and when they allowed me to put my fledgling portfolio in front of them…which they would subsequently bash and crap all over. Now I get to crap all over students' work, and it feels SO good. Not because I'm a sadist or seeking revenge, but because I'm helping them. The fact is, that brutal feedback I received as a student is exactly what pushed me to work harder and get better.

Another important thing that gives me some cred is that I actually love being an ad creative. I've found as I've gotten older and been around a lot of folks who work in various careers, that loving your job is a rare thing. I'm a lucky guy. I've had plenty of sleepless nights over the work I'm doing, but not a lot of sleepless nights thinking, "What the hell am I going to do with my life?" This is more than a job for me. It's a passion. I think being an advertising creative is absolutely bad ass, and my hope is that this book gives you the information you need to be totally convinced you're going to love it too (or totally freaked out and convinced you'd hate it, which is okay too).

Enough about me. If you're convinced I've got something to teach you, let's get on with it.

WHAT? SOME EXPECTATIONS FROM THIS BOOK.

So, I'll tell you right off the bat, this isn't exactly one of those "how to get into advertising" books. I mean, it sort of is, but not exactly. It's more of a, "so you think you may want to become one of those people who makes ads for a living? Here's WHAT you need to know before you really get down to work making that happen" book. Consider it a prequel to the "how to" book. This will make more sense once I start going into details about portfolios.

I believe the term, "look before you leap" is a really appropriate one. This book will give you a good look, some good info on what the leap entails, and some valuable tips on making your leap a non-disastrous one. And if you're thinking, "wow, I just paid $X for this book and I'm not even going to learn how to do anything," bare with me. There are some good reasons I felt it was more important to write a book that's much more about the what than the how to.

First off, going for a job as an ad creative isn't your usual career pursuit. By that I mean that you don't go to college, get a degree, send around your resume and hope to get a gig. It's much more involved than that. There's a lot to learn before you even start the pursuit.

Second, it's my professional opinion, with all due respect to the how to books out there, that a book isn't the best place to get the how to, so I certainly wasn't going to write one. But a pretty short book that let's people know what they need to know about getting a job as an ad creative? I felt there was a need. Also, I think that beyond just helping you come to a decision on whether you actually want to try going for a gig as an ad creative, supplying you with the what, will help you be more successful if you do decide to move on to the how to.

For example, there's a reason you sit in a classroom, bored out of your hormone-drenched 15-year-old skull, learning about traffic signs and stuff before they throw your unprepared ass behind a steering wheel and start to teach you how to drive (not to suggest that this book is going to be boring, like a driver's ed class. At least I hope not.). If you understand *what's* out there before you before you learn *how to* drive, your chances of driving off the side of the road, or worse, are much lower.

You want the *what*. You need the *what*.

Now, I should elaborate a little bit on the statement that there's no *how to* in these pages. There are some sections that will feel a lot like I'm teaching you how to build the portfolio of work you're going to need to get a job. But they're more about revealing stuff that will be expected of you as an ad student.

Another reason for a driver's ed class also helps put you in the right mindset to get out there on the road. It isn't just facts, it's mental preparation. Which brings me to another thing I hope you take away from this book. I've written it in a way that will help put you in that oh-so-important right mindset.

Being mentally prepared is obviously pretty helpful should you choose to take on the task of getting an ad job. Let this be the first of many times I'm going to mention this: though it's often a fun and satisfying pursuit, getting a job as an ad creative is an all-consuming and difficult emotional roller coaster. It can be like a relationship that most of the time doesn't feel like it's working, but those snippets of bliss let you know is worth fighting for. Or maybe it's not. That will be up to you. I really want to not only reveal the details of the mental battle, but also give you some tips on how to best deal with the highs and lows you will—not might—will experience. As an instructor who has taught hundreds, no thousands (okay, hundreds), of student ad creatives the how to, I've had many many students come into their first semester without the mental preparation. The results can be ugly. They get their asses kicked by the brain strain of the how to. I just think to myself, "Oh, you poor little soul. You just had no idea what you were in for, did you, kid?

So, suffice it to say, you will not finish this book and be working at an ad agency in a jiffy. Actually, you won't finish this book and be anywhere close to getting a job as an adverting creative. Not because this book sucks, but because it just doesn't happen that way. You'll be closer, but not close. It's a long journey, friends. But what I will offer you is that you will finish this book and be much better prepared to take on a very difficult task, and this will lead you greater success in that task.

To sum it up in a simple way: this book explains what you'll eventually need to know how to do, but not the how (not in-depth how, anyway), just the what—that is if you really want to get to the how.

What?

I just did that for my own amusement. Get used to it. If I can't entertain myself a little bit while I'm helping you people out, I'll never finish this thing. Writing a book is hard.

A QUICK, WORD ABOUT THE CRAPPY ILLUSTRATIONS AND HANDWRITTEN STUFF

I actually had photos to help illustrate various stuff I talk about in this book, especially some of the sample ad campaigns. But honestly, I don't know how all the photo rights and legal usage junk works, so I was kind of nervous about using them. Then a solution hit me. There's a pretty rock solid truth about concepting ideas for ads (especially print ads): if a concept is good, you should be able to successfully communicate that idea with a handwritten headline and rough sketch—even a poorly drawn one, which is good, since most people can't draw that well. In fact, as I'll talk about later, even in these days of fast computers and instant access to limitless images through a simple Google search, my experience is that the majority of ad concepts still start out as Sharpie ink on a piece of printer paper. So I thought, hey, I'll just sketch this stuff out myself. After all, most of these campaign examples probably started out that way. Problem solved.

GLOSSARY OF TERMS

*U*sually glossaries are in the back of a book. But in this case, I think it might serve you better to have it in the front. The reason is that there are some terms that I think will be helpful to have at least a slight understanding of from the get go. I'll be getting much deeper into all the stuff laid out in this glossary later, but I like the idea of having your pump primed with these words swimming around in your head. Okay, enough with the slightly unpleasant sounding metaphors.

And yes, I know they're not in alphabetical order. They're in Andy's Perceived Order of Importance.

Portfolio, aka Book, Student Book, Student Portfolio, Portfolio Site (I switch back and forth, and so do people in the industry, so learn all of them): A collection of spec (see definition below) ad campaigns you've created. When it comes to getting a job as an advertising creative, your portfolio isn't an important thing, it's the only thing. As I mentioned earlier, this is not an industry that relies much on resumes. Your student portfolio is what you'll show to prospective employers. You absolutely won't get a job as a creative without a portfolio, so if you decide to pursue this career, you will be making one. This book could have easily been called "What you need to know about building a student portfolio." It's probably at least mentioned on every page.

Spec Ads (short for speculative): Obviously when you're a student, you're not working at an ad agency, so you don't have clients. So how do you put together a portfolio to show off how good you are at making ads? Well, you fake it. For reals. You pick a product or service, pretend that you're an ad creative, and do a spec campaign for it. Then you pick another product or service, and you do another spec campaign. And so on. Simple, right? Simple to understand, yes. Simple to do, not really. Simple to do well enough to get a job as an ad creative, (just imagine me laughing).

Media (plural)/ Medium (singular): I just want to make sure that you know when I use this word, "media," I'm not talking about the news media. I'm talking about forms of media. For example, TV is a medium. Magazines and newspapers are forms of media. For our purposes, I usually use media/medium in terms of what type of media an ad in your portfolio would be placed in: web ad, print ad, etc. The singular/plural uses are a bit funky, and most people don't use the singular "medium" at all. I'll try to keep it straight, but I don't make any promises I'll use it correctly since I write pretty conversationally. I actually had a mass communications professor in school who used to say "the media are powerful." It was just weird sounding.

Advertising Creative, AKA Ad Creative, or Creative: The plural form of this word, "creatives," still drives Microsoft Word nuts, and makes it go all red-squiggly-line on me, but screw MS Word—in the ad world, it's a word, dammit. A Creative is what you're thinking about becoming if you're reading this book. There are several different levels of creatives, but basically there are three creative positions: art directors, copywriters and creative directors (definitions below). An art director and a copywriter will normally work together as a team to come up with ideas for ads. A creative director is their boss.

Art Director: The part of the creative team who is a bit more savvy on the visual end of ad creation. An art director has to be very proficient, preferably an expert, in the graphics programs, like Adobe Creative Suite, and should also know their stuff a bit when it comes to web development.

Copywriter: The part of the creative team who specializes in writing ad copy (the words on an ad). A copywriter is usually the person behind headlines or taglines on billboards, print ads, web stuff and responsible for writing TV spot scripts (that's not to say the art director doesn't come up with ideas for TV spots, but the copywriter is usually the one who has to put together the script). Usage example: Andy Beach is a bald copywriter.

Partner: Your creative partner (the art director you work with if you're a copywriter or the copywriter you work with if you're an art director) is usually called, well, your "Partner." Makes sense, but it really is kind of a vernacular-type word in the ad world. If you're a dude, you can be at an ad industry party and say, "Oh, you're Mike Thomas? I think you know your partner, Scott," and no one will think anyone is talking anyone's boyfriend. Not that there'd be anything wrong with Mike and Scott being more than work partners, though office relationships can be complicated and are normally frowned upon.

Art School, AKA Portfolio School: THIS is the place I recommend you get the aforementioned how to, and I'll talk more about them at length later. Seems kind of weird, but there are actually schools out there that specialize in helping aspiring ad creatives build their portfolios in preparation for getting a job. Actually, there are quite a few of them. Most art schools are two-year post-grad programs where you leave with a certificate of completion and your (hopefully) completed portfolio, but a few actually offer Master of Fine Art degrees in advertising if you want to go as far as get a Masters. When you're a student at one of these schools, you essentially act like you're a creative at an ad agency. You come up with a bunch of ideas for spec ad campaigns, and the instructors, usually professionals, like myself, act like creative directors. The best stuff ends up in your portfolio. The bad stuff (and you'll make a ton of it) ends up in the recycling bin. I should mention that there are also some undergrad programs out there that you can start right after high school, like at the Academy of Art University, where you'll get all the general education stuff all college students have to take. But this book is talking more to folks who have graduated from college or are on that track. That's not to say this book won't be useful if that's not you. It will be, it's just not going to feel like I'm talking specifically to you all the time.

Andy Beach

PART II:
ABOUT THE INDUSTRY

FIRST THING'S FIRST: WHO MAKES ADS, ANYWAY, AND HOW DO THEY DO IT?

*U*nless you've already done a bit of research, your experience with the creation of advertising has probably been through TV and movies. Not surprisingly, movies and TV shows normally get it fairly wrong (as they do when portraying most real world, non-superhero professions. But seeing how watching most people work isn't the most enthralling activity, I understand why artistic license is necessary). Even "Mad Men," which is a great show that's often praised for its authenticity, isn't the best source for accurate info on how a modern advertising agency works because obviously it's not about a modern ad agency Which is a good thing if you're a woman, minority, non-smoker or, well let's face it, anything other than a hard drinking, secretary-butt-patting white male. Real life in the ad agency world is also not like *What Women Want*, which showed Mel Gibson trying to come up with ideas to win the Nike Women's account all by himself. When you finally do break into the ad world, you'll see that Mel being able to read women's minds was actually the *second* most unrealistic thing in that movie: advertising is a big time team effort, especially in a giant new business pitch.

I could go on and on and debunk movie after movie and TV show after TV show that poorly represent what goes into making ads. But it'll just bore you and, in the process, cause me to date myself by bringing up shows that may have been on before you were born.

But while we're on the subject, I will bring up a little entertainment-related digression that may interest you if you think big.

There's a reason the ad industry often shows up in TV shows, movies, and books: the entertainment industry is absolutely packed with people who started their careers writing, directing, filming, photographing, producing or acting in (guess. go ahead, guess) advertisements!

The list of massively successful entertainment people who started out in advertising is endless. The list is also super sexy, incredibly wealthy, goes to the sweetest parties and hooks up with models. So if you've had thoughts of working in the entertainment industry, the ad industry is a pretty decent place to start. It truly does give you a foot in the door. You get to know people. Personally, I've never thought of the ad industry as a steppingstone, but if I did decide I wanted to try my hand at writing a screenplay, I'd actually have some people in L.A. that I could contact.

The ad world's connection to the entertainment world is something to be kind of excited about, and not just because you may possibly have some pretty cool career opportunities beyond advertising. As a creative person, you should get geeked by the fact that you're going to get to work in an industry with a lot of super-talented, incredibly creative, and highly driven people. It's rad to see people I've collaborated with go on to become well-known actors and directors. The people I have the privilege of working with (and not just the people who have gone on to "bigger" things) are one of the aspects of my job that I enjoy the most.

Anyway, back to what I was saying about your exposure to the world of advertising through the media: forget what you've seen in the theaters and on TV. Your friend and mine, Andy Beach, is going to tell you who really makes ads and what process they follow. From that, you can start to think about which position would work best for you.

THE POSITIONS

There are actually only two positions that you need to concern yourselves with at this time: *copywriter* (like me) and *art director*. More specifically, the positions you'll be shooting for are *junior* copywriter or *junior* art director. "Junior" isn't the most flattering modifier, but it beats "rookie" or "slack-jawed greenhorn."

Art directors and copywriters almost always work together in teams of two: one art director and one copywriter. It can vary, but not often. A lot of times agencies will even hire a team that has worked together at another agency or even a junior team that has worked together a lot in art school and hit the job market together.

So what are the differences between an art director and copywriter? Well, since you're a smart person, you can probably figure out quite a bit simply by their titles. However, there is some further explanation needed.

I'll start by saying that in the ad agency world, the main role of the art director and copywriter is a shared one: come up with ideas, aka "concepts," for ad campaigns. The copywriter and art director will bring their own individual talents to the table when it comes to coming up with ad concepts, but it isn't until those ad concepts are being produced into real live ads that art director and copywriter really do what their titles say. However, and I can't stress this point enough, the *whole process* of making ads is very much a team effort. It's extremely important that you go into this whole ad-making thing with confidence in your individual abilities and ideas, but also with confidence in your ability to collaborate. Unless you're insanely talented, the ad world has very little tolerance for the lone wolf (also known as, "a thick headed a-hole"). And if you're an unproven junior creative, the ad world has *zero* tolerance for that kind of attitude.

So, as you've probably already figured out, when it comes to executing the ads after the concepts have been thought of as a team, the copywriter will take the lead on the words. This includes writing headlines, body copy, and taglines on magazine print ads, web banners, outdoor billboards, or anywhere else stuff needs to be written. The copywriter is also responsible for writing the scripts for broadcast spots, like TV spots, radio spots, pre-movie cinema spots, and spots on the web. But did I mention that both copywriter and art director come up with ideas for all these ads together? I told you I couldn't stress that point enough, but this is the last time, I swear. Actually, I can't promise that.

The copywriter will also normally take the lead in directing the voice talent during studio recording sessions for broadcast voice overs (any voice you hear during a spot that isn't coming from an on-screen actor) and radio spots. At shoots for broadcast spots, the copywriter and art director are both on set to protect the integrity of your collective vision for the spot, but the copywriter will usually be the one to make on-set changes to the dialogue, if necessary. But even those things are usually done with your partner by your side. Go TEAM!

The art director (surprise surprise) takes the lead on the visual aspects of making ads. The art director designs the layout of print ads, web banners or billboards and will also go to photo shoots to help direct and collaborate with the photographer. Suffice it to say, if you want to become an art director, you need to be a good graphic designer and very proficient and skilled in design programs. At broadcast shoots the art director, like the writer, make sure the integrity of the spot is being preserved, but also concern themselves a bit more with how the set and wardrobe are looking. The art director will also usually sit in on recording sessions and collaborate with everyone involved, but like I said, it's usually (but not always) the copywriter who takes the lead on directing talent.

So those are the two positions you're shooting for. Yes, there are higher up creative positions like associative creative directors (ACDs), creative directors (CDs) and then the ultimate, big time honchos like executive creative directors (you guessed it, ECDs), but even those people are either copywriters or art directors, and they started out just like everyone else: with "junior" in their title. They've just risen through the ranks. And though they may no longer have "copywriter" or "art director" on their business cards, an individual always kinda holds a special place in their heart for their original specialty.

MAKING THE MAGIC HAPPEN

To describe the roles of the positions a bit deeper and at the same time educate you on the process of making ads, I'm going to set up a hypothetical ad assignment. For the purposes of keeping things simple, this hypothetical assignment is going to go smoothly and without a hitch. But obviously, as any complex task in real life, that's not too realistic. If you get into the ad world, you will find that "smoothly" is a very relative term. Even the easiest assignments will—not might—*will,* run into problems that must be solved.

On with the show.

Because everything is going to go smoothly, we'll call our hypothetical agency Perfecto, Perfecto and Partners (Started by the Perfecto brothers), or 3P, for short.

Let's say 3P's client, Moosh Brand ice cream, wants to start promoting their new line of low fat ice cream.

The first thing that happens (I'm skipping a lot of the strategic and financial stuff that goes on between a client and their agency before a creative assignment is given) is an agency account manager, who has been briefed by the client, will give the **creative director** (your future boss) and the **creative team** (future You and your future partner), or teams, depending on the size of the client and assignment, a **creative briefing** (also called a **download**, which is annoying to me since it's a computer term being applied to human beings).

The short explanation of the creative briefing is that the creative team is given a document called a creative brief (which is a good name for it) and there is discussion on:

1. Who is the target market (for our scenario, it's women, 18-34).

2. What, in simplest terms possible, the client wants to communicate to the target market.

3. Deliverables, which breaks down approximately how big of a campaign the client wants (more specifically, can afford) and what the media is: print, TV, web or a combo (in our scenario, let's say a campaign of 5 print ads to appear in women's magazines) and how much time they have to pull it all off (just a heads up, usually it's less time than is ideal).

4. Other info, like any market research that has been done, that the creative team may need to know in order to come up with effective ads that will help sell carton after carton of ice cream.

After the briefing the creatives can get to work.

So, as I've mentioned, our heroic creative team is at first single-minded in their effort to do one thing: come up with concepts for an ad campaign. Our copywriter may come up with some great visually driven concepts and, in turn, the art director may come up with some cool headlines or taglines. Each brings their own talents, but for the most part, there is no copywriter, there is no art director, there is only a creative team. Damn, I'm getting excited just writing about it! I'm rooting for these guys! Are you? You should be. They're future You!

Okay. I'm settled down now.

As I mentioned at the begining of the book, most, if not all of this concepting happens in a pretty simple way: they sit in a room or in their office or wherever, and put pen to paper. Like, seriously—Sharpie marker and a sketch pad is all we're talking about here. The ad creation world is a complex and technically advanced one these days, but initial ad concepts are thought up the same way today as they were 100 years ago: just thinking and working stuff out and tossing ideas back and forth. You kill ideas that go nowhere and nurture the ones that get you excited.

This period of concepting goes on for…well, however long you're given. But for our purposes, let's say a week. Our heroes toil away, knowing that in a week they've got a date with their boss, a creative director, to show him (there are many female creative directors, but for simplicity's sake, I'm just going to use the masculine. Cool?) the ideas they're working on. As they get closer to this date, the creative team needs to start tightening up their ideas to the point that they look more like ad campaigns. Things are still very rough at this point, but the copywriter needs to start focusing on the written part of the campaign ideas and the art director needs to start drawing things out a little more clearly (don't worry, being great at drawing isn't necessary to be an art director. It helps, but it's not as important as it was in the "Mad Men" days). The team pretty much does whatever they need to do, using their individual skills and talents, to make sure their concepts will be clearly communicated to the creative director. Maybe that includes a little comping up stuff on a computer, but not always. It's all about ideas at this point, not fancy layouts.

I think it's probably a good time to note that the best concepts are the ones that come through loud and clear without fancy photography and digital effects. If you need to do a lengthy explanation to sell your idea to an advertising professional, like a creative director, chances are pretty low that people who will see your ad for the length of time it takes to turn a magazine page are going to understand it.

When the day comes for the team to present their concepts to their creative director, they'll hang their work up on a wall and go through their ideas.

The creative director then directs the team's creative work. Get it? Directs the creative...creative director.

This early in the process, this meeting is more of an informal check in than a make-or-break presentation. Some (actually, most) concepts will be killed on the spot. Some concepts will be viewed as having some hope. The creative director then makes his suggestions to help those "almost" concepts, and will say stuff to the effect of, "Maybe do *this* instead. It also might be cool if you do *that*. Did you try to do *this* to *that*?" And so on. Also, if they're lucky, the team also has one or two ideas that make the creative director say, "Hey, that's great. Keep pushing that idea."

After the review, our gallant team leaves the meeting, either feeling good about themselves, or like they want to jump out of a window, or maybe

somewhere in between. But regardless, they are professionals, so it's time to get back to work. They take the creative director's advice on how to make the surviving work stronger and also continue to come up with new ideas. You can probably guess how it goes from there: more tightening things up and fine-tuning of the work followed by more creative reviews with the creative director. Eventually the account managers (people who work for the agency that are the liaisons between the agency and the client and make sure things stay on schedule and on budget) will sit in on a creative review and give their thoughts as well.

The end goal is to get all the campaign ideas whittled down to roughly three to four (although, once again, it varies from project to project) semi-tight campaigns (remember campaign means a series of ads, and you are coming up with several campaign ideas) to show to the folks at Moosh Brand ice cream in a client presentation. Go time, baby.

A few things can happen at the client presentation:

Things go well and the client really likes one of the campaign ideas and says something like, "Man, you guys are brilliant. It's really hard to choose from all these great ideas, but let's go with that one."

The second thing that can happy is that things go pretty good (this is usually how it goes) and the client says, "These are pretty good and we're happy, but…" followed by some feedback and some collaboration. It's all good, but bottom line, some more concepting and fine-tuning usually has to take place and another client presentation will take place down the road.

Lastly and leastly, things go badly and the client says, "You guys are missing the mark. None of these are working for us at all. Are you guys high or something?" In cases where a client presentation has gone badly, the agency hopes that the client has some good direction and can clearly explain how said mark is being missed, and what it is they're looking for. But bottom line, it's back to the drawing board for the creative team. It's a drag, but it happens to everyone. Sometimes the direction from the client or the account team wasn't clear. Sometimes the creative director steered things in the wrong direction. And sometimes you just kind of suck on a project and don't nail it. It happens.

You just need to make sure you don't let it happen that often and that you bounce back for the next round.

But I want our hypothetical situation to have a happy ending! It's our party, so let's make it a sweet one!

Let's say that the folks at Moosh were blown away by one of 3P's campaign ideas and want to run with it. Woo hoo!

The job of the creative team is now to turn this still somewhat rough campaign idea into a polished, beautiful ad campaign, ready to be printed in women's magazine.

Producing final ads is a process in itself. It involves more revisions and more presentations with more approvals and input from the creative directors and the client. The copywriter writes whatever body copy is needed. The art director oversees any photography needed and designs the layout of the ad on his/her fancy computer. Then there are even more presentations and approvals.

Once final client sign off is given, the layouts are handed over to production artists who build various versions of the ads depending on what size is needed for the various magazines. Files are sent off to magazines and:

TA DAAAAHH!

There they are in all their glory in women's magazines…for people to mostly ignore (let's face it, the vast majority of ads are ignored and avoided at all costs). But since this is our fantasy project, let's say enough people don't ignore the ads, and Moosh makes a good product, and sells a Great Wall of China of cartons, and everyone is happy.

Hopefully by now, you kinda understand how an ad campaign is made and what the two types of ad creatives—copywriter and art director—do. And hopefully you already have a rough idea of which you'd be better suited to do. If not, don't sweat it. We'll talk a bit more about picking one in the next section. And if you *still* don't know, you'll figure it out eventually. Honestly, you've got no choice, and that always helps people make a decision. But it's not as dire as all that. Choosing to be an art director or copywriter isn't as hard as you think. I'll give you some tips in the next section.

COPYWRITER OR ART DIRECTOR? THAT'S A GOOD QUESTION.

To start this section, I'll talk about something I enjoy talking about: Me. That's a little joke, but in this case I think it's a good plan. Back when I found out that there weren't just "ad creatives," but both copywriters and art directors and that I needed to decide which to be, I was a bit perplexed. I didn't know which I wanted to be.

As I stated in the introduction, I had always been a pretty good writer. A lot of my teachers and professors had even said I was an exceptional writer, which made me smile. In school I knew that if the final grade in a course depended heavily on a big term paper, I was most likely going to get a good grade. So, it was an easy choice to be a copywriter, right?

Not exactly.

The thing was, I also was really enjoying learning how to use layout programs. Plus, I'd always been a slightly (very slightly) above average artist and had loved drawing. I enjoyed both aspects of creating an ad—the visual and the verbal—a lot. In fact, I was actually leaning more toward art direction. But then, brainiac that I am, I suddenly grasped the obvious. Let's see:

I'm so-so at drawing and other visually driven arts.

I'm a great writer.

I can struggle my way to a decent graphic layout.

I get an A on the vast majority of writing assignments.

Gee. Maybe I should take a shot at the position that has "writer" in it. OF COURSE I SHOULD BE A FREAKIN' COPYWRITER!

Here's the deal: you already know if you're a good writer or if you're not. You've had years and years of school assignments and hobbies and personal interests to determine it you've got a way with the written word. If you've got an aptitude and a love for crafting language, then being a copywriter is a good choice for you. On the other hand, if you know if you're a great artist, but an average to below average writer, then it stands to reason that being an art director may be right up your alley.

But it's still not always a cut and dry choice. I know art directors who know their way around a headline and probably could have been great copywriters. And I'm not convinced that I couldn't have been a good art director with more training in that area. We artistic folks are just such multi-talented blessings from above that it can often be a tough choice. Sigh.

But I'll give you a bit more info that may help you make a choice.

First off, and this is just my observation, others may disagree, because computers play a huge role in the art director's job, it's my belief that a bigger percentage of people can be good art directors than can be good writers. I think you can learn to be a pretty good art director starting now, but it's a little late in the game to *learn* to be a good writer. Although I should add, being a good *advertising* writer does takes some training and, especially, experience and practice. But bottom line, if you're going to be a good writer, it will have already happened.

I'm going to shut up before I start getting threats from art directors. But I have some proof to back up my statement: I don't have exact numbers, but there are a whole lot more art directors than copywriters. In most classes that I teach student art directors outnumber student copywriters by about 4 to 1, minimum. I've had classes with no copywriters. Most people just like design and layout better than writing. A big reason for that is that fewer people are good at writing, and they know it. There's no shame in it, that's just the way it is. No matter what, I can't slam dunk a ball, and some people no matter what, can't ace a ten-page paper on poet David Ignatow, or more importantly, write great headlines on a consistent basis. So, even if you like the sound of art direction, but you know you're a good writer and don't hate writing, I strongly recommend you go for copywriting. There's far less competition.

If, however, you turn out to be one of those people who just can't decide, you're not screwed. It's not like you float around in purgatory and can't start on your journey to get into the biz until you decide. Obviously you have to decide eventually, but as I described in the previous section, the majority of the work that professional ad professionals isn't copywriting or art directing: it's coming up with concepts for ad campaigns. And, as you're going to find out, that doesn't just go for the ad creative professional, but also for the ad creative student.

Andy Beach

Speaking of being an ad creative student, let's start talking about what it actually means to be an ad creative student, or ad student, for short. Just what is it that an ad student does, anyway?

Becoming an Advertising Creative: Made Terrifying

PART III:
THE PORTFOLIO

THE PORTFOLIO: LIVE IT. LOVE IT. HATE IT. BREATHE IT. DREAM ABOUT IT. DON'T SLEEP BECAUSE OF IT. AND SO ON.

*T*he explanation of what goes into an ad student's education and/or tasks must start out with an explanation of **the portfolio.** I'll start this out with a simple explanation of what a portfolio is, then I'll get into what the portfolio actually *means,* and how, if you choose to become an ad student, it will rule your freakin' existence. Also, just a quick reminder: as I said in the glossary, the terms "book" and "portfolio" are interchangeable, and I switch between the two a lot. This isn't just to be a pain in the ass or lazy, it's because that's the way people talk in the ad world and, in case it wasn't obvious, I write like I talk. Probably in another five to ten years, the term "book" will die as guys like me are replaced with newer, much cheaper models, retire or die, but in the meantime, it's still being used.

For students, your portfolio—or more specifically since you're still pre-career—*student* portfolio, is a collection of spec ad (short for "speculative," but essentially, they're fake ad campaigns for real products) campaigns you've created.

Your portfolio is the key to getting a job as an advertising creative. To use an old sports cliché, it isn't everything, it's the *only* thing.

So why is that? Because being a creative isn't a business of resumes (I know I've said that before, but it bares repeating). It's all about your book. And that goes for the very beginning of your career, the middle of your career, and on up the ladder. It's actually kind of a tough concept to explain to people. It used to drive me nuts when I was trying to get my first gig when people would ask, "You sending your resume around?"

"No," I'd say. "I'm actually working on getting my portfolio into a place where it doesn't totally suck." I'd go on to explain, "I *have* a resume, but ad creatives don't just send out resumes," etc, etc. It's not the usual job hunt, and most people just don't get it. My friends and family knew that I had graduated from college, so that's what people usually do next, right? Start machine-gunning their resumes to every ad agency in town? Sure, if you want to be an account services person or media buyer. But a creative? Nope. You email the URL to your portfolio site. Your resume should be housed there, and you should have a .pdf of your resume handy, but I guarantee you, it's going to be the last thing that gets looked at. And if they don't like the work in your portfolio, your resume won't get looked at at all.

Prospective employers don't really care where you went to school or what degree you have. They want to see how your brain works and how good you are at making ads. I've often said to ad students that prospective employers only use your resume to get your phone number or email address if they like your portfolio and want to call you in for an interview. The resume and work history becomes a bit more important as your career progresses, but if you're reading this book, you don't have a career, so don't worry about it yet.

Hopefully by now, you're figuring out that you've got a long way to go and a lot of work to do until you can get a job making ads. And if you're not, I'll tell you: you've got a long way to go and a lot of work to do until you can get a job making ads. Building a portfolio is really hard, and building a portfolio good enough to get you a job, well, sometimes it's going to seem next to impossible.

But, friends, it's not all doom and gloom.

For one, building your book is an artistic endeavor and, with the right attitude, is really fun. Also, thanks to the massive challenge it poses, seeing it take shape is really satisfying.

Also, when you really think about it, the fact that hiring is based on the quality of an ad creative's book is one of the raddest things about the ad biz. Yes, building your book is a ton of work, and the judging of creativity is highly subjective, which sparks plenty of disagreement and massive frustration for those being judged. But the great news out of the whole scenario is you're not going to lose out on a job to someone who is vastly inferior to you just because they were in the same fraternity as the boss or some other crap like that. That's not to say that getting a job as a creative isn't *aided* by connections. Knowing people helps you get your foot in the door. But if someone's book sucks, only under the most corrupt and lame circumstances is that someone going to get a job over someone whose book rocks. And folks, in the business world, that kind of level playing field is a rare and beautiful thing. It's no secret that utter incompetence can sometimes (actually, more than just sometimes) find its way to the top of the executive ranks. There are people who are really bad at their job, but actually really good at getting promotions. Needless to say, this frustrates the hell out of people who are good at their job but get skipped over by someone who sucks at their job. But in the ad creation world, it's been my experience that that kind of B.S. is refreshingly rare. Personalities and leadership qualities do count for something, but the bodies of work of the top dogs in this business are awe-inspiring with shocking consistency. In other words, if you become a famous creative, it's not because you kissed a ton of ass or find yourself naked in the same room as someone who can promote you. No, you almost always rise to the top because you make great ads when great opportunities present themselves.

So it's my recommendation if you're going to pursue and subsequently achieve a career as an ad creative, you should go ahead and start obsessing and worrying about your portfolio right…about…NOW! And why not? It's the key to how quickly you'll get hired and how good of an agency hires you.

Oh, and here's another good reason you should go ahead and start obsessing about your portfolio now: so you can start getting used to it. You'll be doing it for the vast majority of your career. You don't get your first job and say, "Whew. Glad I'm done with that portfolio thing." You've probably noticed that I've mentioned *my* portfolio (go ahead, check it out. andythewriter.com), and I'm no student. Your student book, full of spec work, will get you your first job. Then once you get that job, you'll need to start filling your book with your best professionally produced work, as well as even more spec work if you happen to come up with some great stuff that doesn't get bought by a client. Then, when you're eventually ready to move on to another agency (or you get laid off or fired, which I can pretty much guarantee will happen to you in your career), you'll use it to get a new gig. The quality of the work in your book also helps determine the size of your paycheck. Yeah, I'd say your portfolio is pretty important.

Let me tell you a little story. About a week into my career I had a grizzled, but incredibly smart, art director named Wally tell me, "Andy, you don't work for the clients. You don't work for this agency. You work for your book." Personally, I've always felt a bit more loyalty toward the agencies that have been good enough to pay me to do something I find fun, but wonderful old Wally's statement about the importance of your book is pretty much spot on. As a professional creative, there's one thought that you have in the back of your mind going into pretty much every assignment: "Hopefully this assignment results in work that's good enough to put in my book." And you'll have a very similar thought as you start each new spec campaign as a student: "I hope I come up with an idea for a campaign that is worth putting in my book."

Not to belabor the point, but as both a student and then a professional, I can say with almost no doubt that you will on occasion suffer portfolio-induced insomnia. You will toss and turn, stare at the ceiling or whatever your personal favorite method of not sleeping is, because you're thinking about the quality of your book (or more specifically, the perceived or actual *lack* of quality, since as I've mentioned creatives are often an insecure bunch). You will also most likely experience some level of self-loathing over procrastinating work on your book. You will also have bouts of beating yourself up for not working *hard enough* on your book. And if you don't experience all the stuff I've described above, you're either a much more calm than most ad creatives I know. That or you need to get an increased sense of what you're up against.

In fact, I'm planning on doing a little tossing and turning over my book tonight. Hell, maybe your first experience with lost sleep will be tonight after you read this. If that's the case, sweet. I've sufficiently done my job. You realize that building your book is serious stuff.

But, like I said, it's also fun!

31

WHAT'S IN A BOOK: INTRO

Now that I've given you an overview of that symbol of self-worth we in the biz call, "my book," and have mercilessly pounded its oxygen-like importance to your career into your malleable brains, let me give you a more detailed idea of its physical form and contents.

The following "What's in a Book" sections are as close as I'm going to get to a *how to build a portfolio* section. I hope you do take some of these tips with you if you decide to pursue a job as an ad creative and build a portfolio, because I think they're good ones. But the main reason for these sections is to give you some expectations on what it's going to take to get your book to the point that it's "hirable." Consider it preparation and mind set stuff, not a step-by-step on how to actually build your book. I'll tell you where to get an education on how to build your book later. I hope it excites you. If it doesn't, well, that may be a good clue that advertising isn't for you, which is fine. As I've stated, this book is also to help people make the decision *not* pursue a career as an ad creative.

WHAT'S IN A BOOK: PART 1
THE FORM

First off, to refresh your memory, the words, "portfolio" and "book" are interchangeable. Also, when I say "book" or "portfolio," just assume I mean your portfolio *website*.

On that note, I'll come right out and say it: unless you're going to pay someone to build it for you, you're going to have to build a website. I'm sure many of you reading this are of the generation for which building a site isn't that big a deal, which is cool. But I'm hoping this book will cater to a lot of second career folks who didn't come out of the womb knowing HTML, so don't be so impatient, junior. Building a site isn't a no-brainer for everyone out there. I know it sure wasn't for your humble author who happened to be born during the Nixon era.

If you're one of those folks thinking, "Hey, I don't know how to build a website. That sounds hard," don't sweat it. It's not nearly as tough these days as it was just a few years ago. Also, you've got no choice, so get used to the idea. You *must must must* have your book in web form. I'll also offer that you should be glad about this. In the olden days, when someone at an ad agency said, "Send me your book," what that actually meant was, "Hey, mail me your printed portfolio—at your expense—so I can throw it in a massive stack of other books that maybe, god help me, some day I'll get through." Then you had to deal with getting it back from them. Those days of unwieldiness are over and good riddance. Getting printed books out was a pain in the ass, and could be really expensive too. Now "send me your book" means "email me the link to your site." Easy money.

And like I said, getting your stuff on that thing they call the World Wide Web is easier now than it's ever been. There are some great programs out there, like Adobe's Dreamweaver, Apple's iWeb (which is part of the iLife software suite for the Mac), and Microsoft FrontPage, just to name a few, that make creating a pretty cool and fancy site pretty easy if you're willing to spend a little time learning how to use them. There are also more and more portfolio template platforms that are hugely popularity. The one that I'd highly recommend is cargocollective.com. As a matter of fact, if you checked out my portfolio, you know what a portfolio running on Cargo looks like. It's pretty much the king of portfolio template platforms. After years of struggling with building a site (which included a lot of begging my web designer friends for help), I finally switched to Cargo. I LOVE Cargo. It's relatively easy (and if you have any web publishing knowledge at all, it's incredibly easy), very clean and saves a ton of work compared to building a site from scratch. Another similar service that's great is carbonmade.com. Some people even just use blogs, like wordpress.com or squarespace.com, to get their stuff online. Some applications and services are more robust than others, but with any of these you can have a site up really quickly. However, I should let you know, the graphical layout, creativity, and overall appeal of your site does count for something, so you may not want to go *too* bare bones. The aesthetics of your site should reflect your personality, even if it's just the writing you do that talks about your work and yourself. Your portfolio site shouldn't just sell your ability, it should sell you.

Now, before I get into what I mean, I should note that that portfolio platforms, like Cargo, have limited customization features, so I'm mostly talking about building a site if you chose to do so. But there are still opportunities to make your portfolio more *you*.

A while back a creative recruiter named Lisa Coris woke me up to the fact that as ad creatives, one of the most important products and/or services we need to brand is ourselves. Essentially, we're like a mini-business. She turned me on to this concept after looking at my book and seeing my work but not much else.

"It always shocks me how a group of people whose job it is to create brands are so bad at branding themselves," said Lisa. "I can see your work, but what's surrounding the work doesn't say anything about you. It needs to."

Wise words.

To give you an analogy, let's say you see an ad campaign. The way it's designed and the tonality of the copy say a lot about the company. If an ad has a ton of bright colors, like on a soft drink ad, it says, "We're fun!" without really spelling it out. On the other hand, an ad for an investment firm sporting a cleaner design and more serious copy says, "We take what we do super seriously, so you can trust us with your money."

Your portfolio needs to do the same thing, and a website just gives you so many more opportunities to do that than a printed book, especially if you take the time to learn a bit more of the technical end of web design. If you have some great ads, and on top of that do some cool design and have some interesting writing on your portfolio site, an agency may be just a little bit more inclined to call you in for an interview. You need to look for whatever edge you can to get noticed. Obviously the work is most important, but if you show just a little bit more flavor than some other creative going for YOUR gig, who knows? It may be the difference between starting your first job and continuing to look for your first job.

I know making your site cool just sounds like more work on top of the massive amount of work that building your book is going to be, but keep the right attitude. If you're a creative person (which I imagine you are, since you're reading a book about getting a job with the words, "creative," "writer" or "art" in them), opportunities to express yourself are *always* a great thing. Creative outlets are why we're on this earth, my artistic brother and/or sister. It should be fun for you, and it's great practice for what you're going to be doing for a living. You will run into your share of frustrations, but I recommend that you enjoy the challenges, even if sometimes it feels like you're forcing yourself to enjoy it. I sure have.

Now I should really stress, *don't go overboard.*

Everyone reading this has enough experience with the web to know what I mean. Fortunately this trend is dying the death it deserves, but there are those sites where you're having to jump through all kinds of Flash effects and crap to get to the information you need. These are the kind of sites that make you think, "C'mon, man! Can't I just get the info I'm looking for without having to watch all your stupid intros and stuff?" Just because you can create some neat little stuff, doesn't mean you should. Always remember, the main function of your site is to show your advertising work. Just like the best advertising, you need to say a lot, but do it in a simple, clean way that's not going to require a bunch of digging and blank or frustrated expressions on the faces of your audience. Prospective employers will just hit that little red dot in the upper left of the browser window (we creatives all use Macs) if they get frustrated with your site, just like you do when you get fed up with an overly complicated or janky site.

Now that I've told you how sweet and all-important portfolio websites are, I should mention that the printed portfolio is not *totally* dead. I don't want you to take all of my ranting about getting a portfolio site built as an indication that you will never have to put together a printed version. There's a chance you will, especially in art school. Sometimes it's nice to have a printed version on hand to take with you to interviews. And there are times it's just much more convenient to have an actual book to go through as opposed to a laptop that you're hoping hooks up to the wi-fi with no issues. You should take it on a case-by-case basis.

Another great use for the printed portfolio is for events called, "portfolio reviews." You'll learn more about them if you choose to go to a portfolio school. At these incredibly nerve-wracking events, you get to move around a room and sit with professional ad creatives and have them review and blast...err, I mean, make constructive comments on, your book. Obviously a laptop isn't always going to be convenient, and I know the day is coming, but we don't all have iPads yet. In our increasingly connected world, this will eventually no longer be the case, but as of right now having a printed version of your book available is still a good idea.

WHAT'S IN A BOOK: PART 2
THE CONTENT

Now that you know what form your book should take, I'll give you some thoughts on what kind of stuff be expected to put *into* a book. Once again, this book isn't designed to help you build a portfolio start to finish, but I think the following stuff will give you a better idea of what you're in for if you decide to pursue an ad job, which this book *is* designed for. But just for kicks, I'll throw in a few portfolio content recommendations to give you some stuff to start thinking about. As a teacher and guy who thinks highly of his knowledge on the subject, I can't help it.

Please note (and I'll give you several reminders of this), there are no set rules or exact numbers involved here. I can only give you an idea of a book's content. And unfortunately there are probably exceptions to almost every recommendation I'm going to make. I'd say that the one rule that rules all rules: if it makes your book stronger, use it. If it makes your book weaker, dump it. It's a pretty subjective rule, but subjectivity rules rule in this business. Make sense? Kinda? Good.

I'm actually going to start with a couple of things that usually *shouldn't* go into your book. Why am I bothering to tell you what shouldn't go into your book? Because these are things I've been asked a lot by students over the years, so I figure I should address them.

First off, don't kill yourself trying to make TV spots and, even more so, don't even think about including scripts for TV spots in your book. Students ask me all the time if I think it's a good idea for them to put a great script for a TV spot they've got in their book. No. No I don't think it's a good idea. End of story. Writing good scripts is hard. *Reading* them is even harder. I should elaborate.

Writing a script that vividly paints a picture of what will be appearing on the screen is difficult. Reading a script and clearly understanding what will be happening on the screen without someone explaining the script in person is even more difficult. Understanding scripts takes multiple read-throughs and a bit of experience. Usually when I share a script with my bosses, it's in the form of a verbal, waving-my-arms-around, doing-my-best-to-act presentation, and I'm usually accompanied by my partner who is doing the same thing. It's like a little play. Also, TV spot scripts, even great ones, are not inherently entertaining to read. That's why creatives have to go all wacky or dramatic in front of their creative directors or the clients to sell them. Getting the picture? Don't put a script in your portfolio.

Now that being said, at some ad schools they will have courses in TV spot development and give you the means to produce a spot. But even if you produce a spot in school, that doesn't necessarily mean you should stick it on your portfolio site. It's extremely difficult to produce a good spot under the best and most professional of circumstances (and I've done plenty of crappy spots to prove that). And when you're totally new at it, well, it's that much harder to produce something worth showing off. If you do produce a cool spot in school that everyone likes, and you truly believe it deserves to be shown, by all means, show it off. But if you do a student spot that doesn't turn out great, which after seeing many student-produced TV spots I can tell you is fairly likely (and that's no knock on the talent of the students), don't put it on your site just because it's there. It'll hurt your portfolio more than it will help it. Bottom line, don't sweat TV. No one is expecting your student portfolio to have a spot.

Another question I get from students is if they should put their other artistic endeavors in their book, like poems, short stories, photography or other art. Back in the printed book days, the answer was the same as the TV script question: No, no and no.

However, the answer to this question has changed a little bit as the portfolio has migrated from printed paper to the web. With printed books, your real estate was limited, so you had room for one thing: ads. In the past some people reviewing your book may have been interested in seeing your sketches or reading your poems, but those people were extremely few and far between. Now with portfolio sites, you can easily have your other artistic endeavors more as optional viewing without distracting from the most important thing in your book, which is (say it with me) ads! Very good, class.

But if you're proud of your other endeavors and want to show them off, go for it. It won't hurt, and in some circumstances, it may possibly help you a little. But keep it *optional*. Just put a link on your site that says, "my art" or something like that. I've even clicked on a few of those kinds of links myself if I found the ads on the site particularly good and I want to see what else the kid was up to. It can add some flavor to your site. Just keep it out of the way of the ads. Always remember you're going for a job as an ad creative, not an illustrator or poet or finger painter, or whatever it is you do.

For example, I've done a bit of mountain biking journalism. I have a mountain biking blog and I've even managed to get a few articles published. So I put a link on my portfolio site: "mountain bike journalism." If someone wants to click it and check out my stuff, cool. Maybe it will make me seem more interesting to them. If they don't care about my creative endeavors beyond my ads, no biggie. The link didn't get in their way.

So, now let's go on to the most commonly asked question: "How many ads do I put in my book?" Since you're a smart person, you probably already know that that's an impossible question to answer on the nose, but I can give you an idea: Around 15-20 pieces. There, now you've got a rough answer. But a more accurate answer would be, don't put too much work in your book, and don't put too little.

The thing is, exact numbers are irrelevant. What's most important is high quality and a good breadth of work. Your book needs to *feel* like it has the right number of pieces in it. You don't want a prospective employer to click through your stuff and think, "Eesh, there's still *more?*" You also don't want people to use the term, "a little thin." I know that probably isn't the most helpful answer, but trust me, once you start building your portfolio and checking out other portfolios, you'll start to get a feel for things.

Let's move past numbers and get you knowledgeable on what I call, "a good range." Let's talk about media mix. Let's talk about the type of work that gets attention. Let's get that brain of yours moving and thinking about what kind of thinking you're capable of. YEAH!

Figuring out what kind of stuff to put in your book is a lot more complicated than it was around the turn of the century when I was trying to get into the biz. The reason being that in the old days, types of media was a really simple thing to talk about. There were print media ads—more specifically spec magazine ads and spec outdoor ads, like billboards and bus shelter ads—and that was about it. Print ads are still incredibly important, but now there's oh-so-much more.

Before I get into the types of ads you can, and should, put in your book, I should clear something up. I'm about to describe the kinds of advertising that in the real world are very difficult to pull off and cost a lot of money to produce. So why would I suggest to you that you come up with these kinds of ideas for your student book when you don't have the means to produce them? Well, because in a way you *can* produce them. You can fake it. With a bit of creativity, maybe a decent digital camera and Photoshop magic, you can absolutely create a very realistic representation of your crazy, creative, and super innovative advertising ideas. In fact, all of the examples of ads I'm about to describe can be adequately represented in a student portfolio with a decent level of proficiency with graphics programs (programs you're going to need to know if you're going to be an ad creative anyway). Sure, in the real world, they're pretty big and expensive undertakings. But when you're building your student book, you're not living in the real world, you're living in the spec world. So if you can think it up, most of the time you can think of a way to pull it off and stick it in your book.

First off, let's talk about digital media. The capabilities of the web, and more specifically for our conversation, advertising on the web, have absolutely exploded the barriers of what we in the ad world can do. Opportunities for creativity are at an all time high, and getting higher, which for people whose job it is to be creative is really exciting.

Recently I've done projects that I never could have even imagined when I started my career, and I haven't really been at it *that* long.

Back in 2000, when I started out as a junior copywriter, we did web banners, but they were incredibly limited and, compared to what's out there today, totally lame. If we were lucky, we got to do an animated banner, you know, one that actually moved! Woweeee!

But today, the world of digital advertising is your creative oyster. Now a banner can expand out and show you a really high quality video with sound. Banners can mess with the content of your web page (for better or for worse). One banner can communicate with other banners. You can play games and interact with banners. I'll stop with all the examples, because I'm sure you've seen it out there. And it's not just ad banners. There are branded viral videos (by "branded" I mean a product or service has a presence), branded interactive games, or fun microsites. You've got YouTube and a million other places you can put videos. YouTube Channels dedicated to one ad campaign are enormously popular. As I write this book, the biggest hit to date is Old Spice's "Man Your Man Could Smell Like" from incredibly awesome agency Wieden+Kennedy.

Beyond those, there's the world of social media, like the epically popular Facebook and Twitter. Advertisers are trying to figure out how the hell to effectively use these to sell product. And in turn, Twitter and Facebook are trying to figure out ways they can help these advertisers so they can sell more advertising space so they can actually make some money. Some cool, creative forms of advertising have already started to appear on Facebook, but there's no telling how it'll be used to sell products in the future. More and more, at the end of TV commercials instead of seeing plain old whatevercompany.com, I'm seeing facebook.com/toyota. People are on Facebook constantly, so that's where advertisers want to be. And I already know that in no time I'm going to have to update this book to include the next big social media craze. Maybe in a few years Facebook will go the way of MySpace, and become irrelevant, with something even cooler replacing it. Who knows, Twitter may be replaced by something actually useful and even more addictive!

Another digital medium is mobile phone apps, especially on the iPhone and Android-based phones. Advertising agencies are cranking out apps for their clients these days, some of them really cool. And of course these mobile apps can be very tied in to social media.

Obviously digital media is huge, and coming up with digital ads is a big part of the ad creative's job, so you absolutely must have a decent amount of spec digital advertising in your book.

Next, getting out of the web world and into the everyday world, there's something called an ambient, guerilla, or alternative media. Alternative to what? Alternative to the media I've just described. Not too long ago web advertising actually fell under alternative media. I'm sure there are still some a lot of books about advertising around that call web stuff "alternative." Does that mean that the stuff I'm calling "alternative media" is going to be mainstream in the next 5 or ten years? Not likely. And you'll see why in a just a minutes.

Alternative media has actually been around forever, but they started getting really cool and popular around 2002 or so.

To give you some examples of some great, game-changing alternative media work I'll tell you about the launch of the Mini Cooper, pulled off by super agency, Crispin Porter + Bogusky (CP+B, for short). You'll hear their name a lot once you start getting more familiar with some of the best, industry changing work because CP+B created a lot of it. Though they're not the creative steam roller they once were, I'd say that shop has had more influence on advertising creative in less time than any agency in history. Some may argue with me, but at this point, it would be tough for them to win.

Anyway, the official message behind the Mini when it launched was, "true exhilaration at an attainable price," because the Mini is pretty zippy and affordable. Personally, what I always took away from the campaign was that *small* is not only more practical, but fun and cool.

One thing to note is that the SUV craze was still in full swing at the time the Mini launched, and gas was still relatively cheap (that is, it wasn't over 4 bucks a gallon). "Small is cool" wasn't a concept that was on many people's mind. "Room for 26 passengers, four-wheel drive, and a 36 cylinder engine! USA! USA!" was closer to the attitude people had when it came to car buying. Needless to say, CP+B and Mini had a Hummer-sized hurdle to overcome.

Another issue to deal with was that the budget was only in the neighborhood of $25 million. To put that in perspective, GM spent about $608 million on advertising in 2002. Oh wait, did I mention that GM spent about $608 million in just the *first quarter* of 2002. Yes, I know GM is advertising several cars, but just trust me, $25 mil ain't a ton of dough in the ad world. So CP+B had to get creative. Fortunately for Mini, they were the guys to do it.

A big TV campaign was out of the question. That would have incinerated that $25 mil. They're semi-common these days, but back when it launched, you may have never seen a Mini Cooper TV spot. A handful were done, but not many, especially for a car company, which are traditionally heavy on TV spots.

So they did some print, outdoor billboards and web stuff (which was also super innovative, and I'll talk about some of it later) but that's where the more traditional media buys, like magazines and billboards, stopped. CP+B and Mini had their thinking caps on. They figured, "Hey, if we do some crazy, highly visible stunts to promote the Mini, I bet people would take notice. And maybe somehow the local news will hear about it. The news always has a couple minutes to fill at the end of the broadcast, so maybe they'll do a story about this weird stunt featuring the Mini. A lot of people watch the news… maybe even some people who want to buy a car! I bet we get some pretty good bang for our buck. Also, I bet a lot of people would take pictures of these kinda crazy stunts and stuff if they saw it, and I'd bet they send the pictures to their friends."

Getting the message? The ad industry sure as hell did. So did the public. These crazy stunts and stuff were a huge hit, and they *were* on the news, and people *did* sent pictures to their friends.

Some examples of these stunts included putting a Mini Cooper on top of a big, unwieldy-by-comparison, SUV and just drove it around town. They also had oversized items built, like giant newspaper machines, phone

booths, and garbage cans, and placed them next to airport ads featuring a Mini with the headline, "Makes Everything Else Seem a Little Too Big." They even made what looked like one of those kiddie horsie rides that they put outside grocery stores, but with a life-sized Mini model on it with the message, "Rides: $16,850" complete with a coin slot.

Then they did a series of stunts called "Mini at the game," where they put a Mini up in the stands with fans. Think it got on TV? You betcha. Think a lot of folks were watching TV? Of course. People *love* TV, especially sports.

Did as many people actually see, in real life, these ambient pieces for Mini compared to a national TV buy? Nope. But how many people actually saw them in the flesh, or plastic or whatever, isn't nearly as relevant as how many people saw them on the news or in the paper or in an email attachment sent from their friend in New York or Chicago. That was some ground breaking thinking, friends, and there's no reason you can't come up with ideas just as cool, mock them up on the computer, and put them in your book. Great alternative media pieces with a great idea behind them gets creative directors really excited.

Another really cool development in advertising relates to good old-fashioned print ads. Huge advances in printing technology and special placements in magazines has opened up the possibilities for what kinds of print work you can come up with for your book. And I'm not just talking about printing and paper quality. What I'm talking about is great advances in the affordability and the do-ability of what are called *inserts* or *spectaculars*.

If you've ever read a magazine, and I'm sure you have, you've come across magazine insert ads. The insert ad, in its most familiar and lame form is the lap flap, or the subscribe-to-this-magazine-for-an-amazing-57%-off-the-newstand-price card, or whatever you want to call it. It's called an insert because it's not glued or stapled in with the pages of the magazine. Inserts are almost always on a thicker stock of paper than the rest of the magazine and are *inserted* using various methods that I won't get into, mostly because I don't know or care about them. Insert ads have been around for a while, but until advances in printing technology, they were insanely expensive to produce.

That's not to say that they're cheap now, but they're much cheaper. Plus a lot of magazines just didn't make inserts an option because they didn't have the means to do it in a cost effective way. But nowadays, it seems that even the smallest circulation magazines can pull off something special if an advertiser has got the dough. The coolest thing is that an insert doesn't even necessarily have to be just paper.

For example, when I worked at Attik in San Francisco, our main client was Scion, the Toyota youth brand of cars. We did a lot of non-traditional, fun stuff like Scion iron-on transfers that we had inserted in magazines, so people could make their own printed tees with Scion graphics. I even did a project where we did an insert that included a nearly paper-thin magnetic sheet of letters. It was even perforated! The idea was that people could tear them out then go out and find a newspaper machine, garbage can, or some other metal thing, and spell out messages, telling the world to F-off or have a nice day or whatever. Just the fact that we could do that is amazing and so much cooler than a regular print ad.

I hope you see where I'm going. *You can think big, folks.* If you come up with a cool idea that involves a piece of fabric with messaging embroidered on it, there's no reason you can't mock it up in Photoshop, or even have it actually made and photograph it for your book. Students do stuff like that.

Just freakin' go for it and have a blast while you're at it. If you have a great idea for an insert that involves sound playing when opened, why not mock it up? How about sound? You can't get a sound chip made, but once again, you can easily represent it in your book, especially now that portfolios are on the web. Record an .mp3 or .wav file of what the insert would sound like and put it on your site. These days, sky's the limit. With the web, and alternative media, you've got a huge range of creative opportunities.

Get excited! Show some range. Be creative!

But also, beware!

All this cool stuff does come with some land mines.

I'll elaborate.

Since about 2004 or so, when campaigns involving web stuff and alternative media became much more common in real life, they become waaay more common in student books.

I don't blame aspiring ad students for jumping into this exciting new world with a lot of enthusiasm. Hell, I just spent the last few pages encouraging you to do crazy and cool stuff beyond the normal print ads so you can show range and creativity. It's shiny and sexy and new and relevant, so of course you *should* do work in these mediums. It also shows that you're knowledgeable about the latest things that are going on out there in the world of advertising.

So what's the problem?

Often when students feature these fancy new mediums in their books I notice the absence of the most important thing: great, super smart concepts. The great concept always has been and always will be king and ruler of all ad creativity. Unfortunately, all these advances in technology and stuff have made recognizing a good ad campaign a bit more difficult for students. More accurately, it's made it harder for them to recognize when they *don't* have a great concept. Poor or so-so ideas can easily be masked by glitz and flair.

I can't tell you how much student work I've had presented to me where the student is saying something like (exaggerated to get my point across and for my own entertainment), "Well, first you get your cell phone, and you send a text message to this big peanut that's laying on a sidewalk, and then you go to a microsite, www.supercoolfreakynuttr27.com, and you go to this page and then you play a Flash game, and if you win you get to pick a character that you can use as your icon on your Facebook page, and if another person who has the same icon sees your icon, you both win a chance to win a trip, but to win the trip you have to see your number…" About quarter into it, my head is spinning.

"What's What is this a campaign for, again?"

"Peanut butter."

And then I drop four simple monosyllabic words: "I. Don't. Get. It."

Then I start asking questions that are probably going to be hard for my beloved student to answer.

"What's the take away for the audience?"

"What are you trying to communicate?"

"What are you telling them about the product?"

"What's the freakin' concept, man?"

Then I say, "I gotta be honest, this idea is just too complicated."

It all comes back to this: just because that kind of wizardry and innovative media exists, doesn't mean it always makes sense to use it. The technology may be cool, but it doesn't make a weak concept strong ("You can't polish a turd," I believe our forefathers said.).

Now let's talk about something that's actually done well: Subservient Chicken. It was done years ago, but still holds up. If you haven't seen it, check it out now. Burger King doesn't host it anymore, but as of this writing you can find it at subservientchicken.com/pre_bk_skinned.swf. It's okay, I'll wait.... have you checked it out? Good. Believe me, the effort and technology that went into building that simple-to-understand little piece was heavy. That poor bastard in the creepy chicken outfit had to perform action after action after action to build up that database of video. He probably sweated off 15 pounds under those lights. But that guy was lucky in comparison to the web developers at The Barbarian Group who had to do the programming to link key words to that database of videos. But the fun and cool consumer facing part of all that work tells such a beautifully simple message: "Chicken your way."

I. Get. It.

And so did everyone else. Super advanced technology went into it, but what the chicken-sandwich-buying world got out of it was a simple, fun, clean and easy-to-understand idea. The result was one of the most successful pieces of advertising in history. Hundreds of millions of people have told that chicken to do whatever lewd thing came to their minds, or just to do a summersault. That's a good use of advanced stuff.

Here's another recommendation I'd make: it may seem contradictory after all my touting of "alternative media," but you should also really embrace print ads like magazine and outdoor billboard ads.

My colleagues and I (aka the people who will be reviewing your student books and deciding whether or not to hire you) have actually discussed our sadness about the declining number of print pieces we're seeing in student books. This absolutely is *not* because we're old farts and miss the old days, at least not me personally. I think I've made it pretty clear how much I love all the advances we've enjoyed in the advertising world. I'm excited to see what the next big thing is going to be. It's cool stuff. But, ignore the simple print ad at your peril.

The greatest thing about print ads is you *can't* mask a weak concept behind a bunch of fluff, at least not as easily as you can with web and other alternative media. That's why I personally think they should make up at least half of your book.

Print is your idea, totally naked, stretched out on the bed, under poor lighting conditions, right after a shower, wearing no make-up or hair product. If it's breathtaking under those circumstances…oh mama. Love the print, friends. It's kind of ironic, but simple print ads are a great way for you to show off your complex, hard-working brains. You can prove that you can come up with a great simple idea that doesn't need to move and dance around. And for you aspiring copywriters out there, if you want to show that you can write some brilliant headlines, print ads are your best friend. And for you aspiring art directors, if you want to show how you are not only a great conceptual thinker but also a great graphic designer who can lay out an ad like nobody's business, say it with me, "print ads." Magazines and newspapers are having a very tough time and are dropping like flies, but they ain't dead yet and, hopefully, won't be for a long time.

To use another, non-naked analogy, you can think of print ads as the low budget indie movie with no special FX that can only be enjoyed if the story and execution are perfect. Sure, there are going to be some yawners that deserve to be forgotten about, but man, when you nail it, it's truly special. Everyone loves those low budget success stories that are successful because they had an irresistible, engaging plot.

Another great thing about working on print is that it actually conditions you and makes you better at coming up with great ideas that *should* be executed with more flash and flair. Using another movie analogy, when you get into creating more complex ad campaigns, you want to create *The Matrix*, not *Transformers*. *The Matrix* (the first one, not the crappy sequels) was a special effects tour de force, but that's not the main reason people loved it. It was an instant classic because the story was so cool. The special FX worked seamlessly alongside the great story to make the entire experience a freakin' knockout. The same thing can be said of a brilliant web execution that has a great idea behind it.

I guess the bottom line is make sure you've got a great idea, no matter what.

WHAT'S IN A BOOK: PART 3
DON'T BE SINGLE MINDED. CAMPAIGNS ARE KING.

The next thing that's really important to understand is that, yes, your portfolio needs to be full of good ads, but more specifically, it needs to be full of good **ad campaigns.**

I guess the first thing we need to get out of the way for this section is that you truly understand what an ad campaign actually is.

Explaining exactly what qualifies as a campaign is surprisingly tough, so I'll give you some nice examples of ad campaigns below. You'll also start to get a feel for what constitutes a campaign when you start looking at advertising award books and other people's portfolios (which I'll talk more about later). But in a nutshell, an ad campaign is a series of ads, be it print, TV, web or combinations of all media, that are all held together by a concept and/or tagline, spokesman, tonality of headlines, art direction, or combinations of all of those.

One example is the classic and endless Absolut Vodka print ad campaign that everyone has seen, (if you haven't, wake up, and then Google it) from TBWA/Chiat/Day, New York. It's been running so long and has been such a hit that there's a coffee table book featuring hundreds of the ads from the campaign. "The Absolut Book" reads very much like an art book, because frankly, the ads are art. Yes, in this guy's opinion, ads can absolutely (no pun intended) be art. Anyway, the commonality that holds this campaign together is that every single ad shows the bottle in one relevant form or another and has the headline, "Absolut (fill in artist, culture, current event, etc. here)," relating to the form of the bottle. It's a wonderful print campaign.

So why the emphasis on campaigns? There're a couple reasons. First off, that's usually what you're going to be trying to come up with once you're working at an ad agency. Second, and most importantly, you need to show perspective employers that you're not only creative, but can think strategically and come up with big ideas that have, as we like to say in the ad world, "legs." When we say "legs," we mean there's a fertile enough idea in play that multiple ads can be made from that one big idea. They can run for a long time. Legs. Get it?

When you're working on building your book, you can't just come up with one ad and call it a day. Those are called "one offs," and except under the rarest of circumstances, one offs don't belong in your book. You need campaigns, campaigns, and more campaigns that show you're brains are full of big ideas, big ideas and more big ideas.

Since pretending is so fun, here's another scenario to give you some elaboration on what I mean by a big idea with legs:

Let's go back to our Absolut ads. I'm sure the real story of how the campaign came about is in "The Absolut Book," but, as I said, I like to pretend. So, what was the one big idea that the creative folks at Chiat/Day came up with decades ago that was so good that the campaign is still running today? What does a big idea look like before it's turned into a long running campaign? Who knows what actually was, but here's some of the kind of stuff that may have been on the brief.

Product: Absolut Vodka

Target Market: Young, somewhat affluent, or "on their way up" males and females, aged 25-45. They are sophisticated, intelligent and interested in art and culture and enjoy social drinking with like-minded individuals.

One thing to say: Absolut is the premium vodka brand for sophisticated people.

Deliverable: Print magazine campaign (number of ads TBD)

With creative brief in hand, the creative teams got to work. One of the teams struck gold. The big idea: "We play on the product name, "Absolut," and use it as an adjective. Then we get hip, well-known artists that our target market is likely to be aware of to do their own artistic interpretation of the bottle. It'll make our product look as equally hip and artsy, and make for some eye-catching ads. We could do a whole bunch of them!"

And that's kind of it. Then they probably just had a few rough sketches of ads to give examples of what they meant.

Did the creation of one of the most famous ad campaigns in history go down exactly like that? Doubtful. But hopefully you get what I mean by "a big idea," in its rawest form. There have been hundreds, maybe thousands of Absolut ads, and they all came from that one big idea. The campaign has expanded beyond just art to cultural events, and politics, and on and on (you'll have to check out the book), but it started with ads like the ones below, that featured artists.

How about Subservient Chicken? What was the big idea behind that? "We come up with a character called 'The Subservient Chicken.' This chicken does whatever people tell it to and have the tagline be something like, 'Chicken Sandwiches Your Way."

I'm over simplifying, of course. Most of the time a bit more crafting and development goes into a great idea, but essentially, that's how all the best campaigns start out: One simple idea with legs.

Big ideas, folks. Not little, stunted ideas with no legs. Big ideas with legs for days.

I also want to elaborate on what's called an **integrated campaign**. Simply put, these are ad campaigns that utilize multiple types of media. Most big ad campaigns are integrated campaigns. For an example, let's go back to our Subservient Chicken (sorry if you're getting sick of him). I've been mostly talking about the microsite where you told the chicken what to do, but Subservient Chicken wasn't just the microsite. It used multiple medium types to convey the message, "chicken your way" and to promote the microsite. There were also TV spots which were funny, but, honestly, really creepy, (you can find them on YouTube) where a young guy told the same chicken from the microsite what to do in a really sensual (if you want to call it that) way. There were also print ads and web banners.

Integrated campaigns are really good to have in your book (without the TV spots, of course). When pulled off well, they definitely show that you can think big.

But, I want to harken back to my warning about potential landmines with all these cool new media: just because you can, should you? When you do an integrated campaign, you need to show how your big idea can fully take advantage of the unique capabilities of each medium, that is, there should be a *reason* that you use a particular medium.

I'll give you an example of what I mean by "just because you can, should you?" I'll give the chicken a rest and use the Absolut campaign.

Let's say I'm an ad creative student building my student book, and I came up with the Absolut campaign. I'm thinking to myself, "Hey, that's a pretty good campaign. I should show what a big idea it is by expanding it into an integrated campaign and make some web banners."

So I jump on my computer and take the images and text from my print ad files and convert them to web banner size. Maybe I'm even good enough on my computer that can animate the banners a little. So I make the bottle come down from the top and the type come in from the left, and boom: a web execution for my sweet Absolut campaign! Now I've got an integrated campaign, right? Wellll, yeaahhhh, kindaaaa. But, that's not necessarily the best use of space in your book. Does this *really* show a great example of how your awesome, big campaign can fully utilize the capabilities of the web?

Not really. When you think about it, you just made your print ads smaller, which is redundant. Even if you do different headlines and have different art on the web banners, you've still got the same issue. You haven't pushed things enough and haven't really taken advantage of what the web has to offer.

Here's a more fleshed out thought to give you an example of *pushing things*: Let's say you mock up a microsite (I say, "mock up" because as an ad student, you're hardly going to have to know how to execute what I'm about to describe. Being able to build such things is a highly specialized gig). Let's call the microsite absoluteyou.com. Or maybe we make it a Facebook app. Yeah, let's make it a Facebook app. And let's say this app lets people create their own Absolut ads using an easy-to-use palette. Neato! Using virtual paintbrushes and maybe some decorations, they get to make their very own special, artistic Absolut bottle! Then they could enter their name and it will create the headline on the bottom of the ad…just as if they were one of the bad ass artists whose art has been featured in the actual ads.

Move over Absolut Picasso, and make way for Absolut Andy!

Then they could print out the piece and have their very own Absolut ad that they could hang in their cubicle or dorm room. And on top of that, they could post the ad they did on their Facebook page with the message, "Look at this cool Absolut ad I made. Click here and you can do your own!" Now it's viral. Now people are interacting with the brand in a really fun way. Now people are passing on the results of those interactions to their friends, who will hopefully interact with the brand themselves! Hey, that's super neato! I love it!

I'm sure you see where I'm headed. This execution can *only* be done on the web, so it more successfully shows how I, ad creative student, can expand a big idea to the web. The first execution, the plain old web banners I described, only shows that I, ad creative student, can use Photoshop and Flash, and that I'm being kinda lazy and not working as hard as I should be. Just sayin'.

WHAT'S IN A BOOK: PART 4
DEVELOP A GOOD EYE

I've spent quite a few pages telling you that to get a job as an advertising creative you need to build a good book. I've even given you some ideas about what kinds of stuff goes into a good book, you know, like good ads. But I've also hinted at some of the frustrations that can be born out of the fact that you will be subjected to some pretty varying opinions (including your own) when it comes to the quality of your work. Which lands us at our next discussion.

How the hell do you tell what *good* ads looks like, or more specifically and relevant to our conversation, how can you tell if the ads in your book are the kinds of ads that are going make a perspective employer say, "Hey, now that's some good stuff! I want to hire this person!"

Before I go on, I want to acknowledge that a lot of this stuff may sound obvious to the point that you may even sarcastically think, "Wow, genius, so you're saying that I need to get better at recognizing good ads before I get a job creating ads? Quite an insight there, Guru Andy. Real glad I bought this book." And although I'd appreciate your sarcasm, it's been my experience with students that it's not as clear as all that. The main reason your judgment of "good" may be off is that you actually *do* have a ton of experience with advertising, but it's not good experience.

You see, we're absolutely inundated with average, run-of-the-mill, nothing-to-write-home-about advertising. No, saying most of my and my colleagues' work is, at best, average, is not a sparkling endorsement, but it's not a sentiment that my beloved industry would argue with. I mean, how are they going to argue? Watch TV for five minutes. Look through a magazine. Most ads are seriously weak. We professionals spend the majority of our time producing average, and often bad, work. That's just the way it is. The good stuff is hard to come by, which is what makes the good stuff sooo freakin' good. But this certainly presents an unexpected challenge to folks like you who are coming in from the outside world. The fact is, inexperienced folks, like yourself, don't know what really great advertising looks like, which makes it pretty tough to create.

You may be saying, "*Whatever,* dude. I know the difference between a good ad and a bad one." Ummm, experience as an instructor tells me that no, no you don't. Not to the level that you need to, anyway.

My first year students consistently turn out ads that are very much like the ads that we see everyday in the real world. That is, they're pretty average. They're not *overtly* bad, but they're just…ads. The more experienced students turn out ads that are better-than-average to good and, occasionally, even great. Obviously this comes through hard work and practice, but just as importantly, it comes through developing an eye for good work. It's pretty obvious why: once they get the eye, they can recognize what's good amongst the work they're producing.

Before I go on, I should elaborate on what I mean by "good advertising" in an ad professional's context.

In advertising, like any artistic industry, there exists a disparity of what is impressive to the experienced professional and the layman, i.e. Joe Schmoe on the street or, well, You—at least You in your present form. I've had many experiences where I overhear people having a conversation about a commercial that they think is so great and funny, and I want to say, "You like *that* spot? Really?" But I hold my tongue. For one, I don't want to get beat up. Also that's kind of a jerky and condescending thing to say. I understand that, as a professional in the ad trade, I have a different standard. It doesn't mean they're dumb. In fact, they may have expertise and standards in their own area that I sure as hell wouldn't understand.

At this point you may be thinking, "Well, the ads are made to communicate with joe schmoe, so if that guy on the bus likes the ad, then it's doing its job."

Yes, that may be the case. But I'm not necessarily taking about real world effectiveness of an ad. I'm talking about something else, so stop interrupting.

We folks who eat, sleep, and breathe the creation of advertising just have different standards. And we should. And if you want to get into the ad game, you should too. You need to forget about what impressed you when you were Joe Schmoe and snob it up. You need to get the eye. Get critical. Otherwise you'll never impress other folks who have the eye, like future bosses. Once you start to recognize the kind of stuff that grabs the attention of professionals, the stuff you're creating as a student will reflect those higher standards. Then one of those future bosses will want to hire you and become your current boss.

So how is that eye developed? Experience is the obvious answer and of course over the long haul, just making ad after ad is going to make the biggest difference. But how do you get that ball rolling when you're a student and just starting out? Well, right now you're inundated with average to below average work, sprinkled with some occasional good work and that's what's formed your opinion of the quality of advertising. So instead why not inundate yourself with good to great work? Easier said than done, right? Actually, the good news is that there are tons of resources that will help you do that. Fortunately for students trying to develop a good eye, we ad folks love to celebrate and congratulate each other (and even more so, ourselves). Because good work is so rare, we like to give it some recognition when it happens…a lot of recognition.

We've got award show after award show. Then we've got books and more books that show the ads that won those award shows. And we've got magazines. All those magazines have websites. Oh yeah, then there are some other websites. There's even a cool magazine that's dedicated entirely to the best student work. All this self-congratulation is a great resource for you as an aspiring creative. You can actually think of them as your textbooks. And unlike actual textbooks, these magazines and sites are always up to date and reflect what's going on at the moment, not what was going on a few years ago, which in the ad business is an eternity.

Back when I was trying to develop my student portfolio on my own, things didn't really click until I discovered and started devouring all these resources. Eventually, I actually started to create some work that didn't totally suck because I finally had an idea of what work that doesn't suck looks like. I distinctly remember an art director reviewing some of my early student work and saying, "This stuff is okay. I can see a client buying this and it running in a magazine. But your portfolio needs to be better than that." After I discovered award books, like the Communication Arts Advertising Annual, I started to figure out what he meant.

The more you see these beautiful collections of the cream of the crop, the more you'll start to get a feel for what kind of work gets recognized. Then you'll be able to rip them off.

Rip off? That's a joke, right?

Nope. It's no joke, and it's certainly what I did when I was a student. Don't worry, I'm leading you to a good place with this, and it's not, "plagiarize your way to the top." I swear.

Actually, "rip off" isn't exactly what I mean. Let's use the term "imitate." Or maybe, "emulate." It's all part of developing a good eye.

To elaborate, let's take a quick look at childhood development. More specifically, let's do an over-simplified analysis of learning to talk.

When we first start putting words together, mostly what we're doing is imitating what we hear over and over again. You've got mom and dad all up in your grille repeating, "Mama" and "Dada" over and over again, so more often than not those, or some other word we hear a lot, end up being our first words. Then we hear more, and we imitate more. Then we start to understand what we're imitating. We understand more, and eventually we're able to form sentences. From this understanding, we're eventually able to get more critical of what is being said. Even our critical abilities are at first imitations. Our opinions, for better or for worse, are at first the same as the opinions of those around us that we look up to: our parents and teachers and the people we like. But eventually from our own experiences, we're able to come up with our own original thoughts and ideas. From there, the impact that our original thoughts and ideas have on others depends on a lot of things, like education, hard work, natural intelligence, and variables like that. But it all starts from us imitating. It's just how we humans learn.

It's like that with a lot of things that we learn to do. No one picks up a guitar and immediately rips out a jam so hot that it causes chicks to flash them. Even the best guitarists learned to play by first painfully picking their way through "Iron Man" or some other well known, yet easily learned riff. Then they get better and better at imitating. Then they start to add their own embellishments and flurries. Then, as they start to really get a feel for what the guitar can do, they start to come up with their own stuff.

It's a process, and it's a process that absolutely holds true in learning to create great ads. These aren't perfect analogies because I'm not saying it's totally cool if you do an exact copy of a campaign, but you know what I mean. You start out by emulating. Then you learn to do your own thing.

As an instructor, I don't mind so much if at first my students come in with work that is derivative of work that I've seen before as long as it's derivative of *good* work. Sure, that student isn't doing totally original work, and I'll point out similarities to existing work because you don't want to have work that's too similar to well-known work in your book. But it's all good because I know that the student is developing an eye for good work, and is heading in the right direction. Eventually, with a lot of hard work, that student's work is going to not only get better, but also more original.

We've touched a little on how difficult the building of a good portfolio can be because of that nasty and frustrating "eyes of the beholder" thing. One person reviewing your book will say, "Wow, I really like this stuff," while another won't think much of it at all. But a funny thing happens as you develop an eye and you get better: the quality of work becomes *less* subjective. There are ad campaigns out there whose high quality is almost unanimously agreed upon amongst professionals. And I'm not just talking about professionally produced work. There are student campaigns of that caliber as well. I've reviewed hundreds of pieces of student work from folks trying to break into the industry, and there are campaigns that make my colleagues and I say,

"Daaaammmn," and then secretly tell ourselves, "I just got served. That punk kid's work pulls down my britches and taunts me. I need to up my game."

One more quick comment about immersing yourself in all these award books, magazines and other sources of inspiration: it's a way to feel like you're in the business before you're in the business, which is important. The more you feel like you're a part of a community, the more motivated you feel. When you're checking out all these ads, you'll notice that they're accompanied by agency and creative team credits. You'll learn which agencies are consistently doing the best work. You'll start to learn some of the big names in the industry. I've mentioned a few of these great shops: Crispin Porter + Bogusky, Wieden + Kennedy and Chiat/Day, but there are so many more. Some are big global agencies, some are small independent shops who have managed to get themselves a good client and are doing breakthrough work. You absolutely should know who is who in the industry. If you see a campaign you love, find out who did it. It's all part of your education. Inevitably you're going to be asked in an interview which campaigns you've seen recently that you like. If you can not only spout off some great campaigns, but also throw in which agency did the work, it makes a really good impression. You should be able to talk shop before you're officially a professional. And honestly, this is advice that I shouldn't really have to give. If you've got the level of passion for the business that you're going to need to break into advertising, you'll *crave* this knowledge.

I won't leave you hangin'. Below are some of the magazines and stuff to look at. A Google search for "award winning advertising" or "world's best advertising" or something like that will turn up a lot of stuff, too. How much does the web rock?

SOME GOOD SOURCES FOR BETTER THAN AVERAGE ADS, AND EVEN SOME GREAT ADS:

Luerzer's Archive Magazine: Pretty cool bi-monthly that you can get at most of the big bookstores or online. It features mostly international ads, which don't always stylistically or conceptually translate that well in America (although, hopefully people from all over the world are reading this book), but you'll see a lot of trippy, boundary pushing stuff in Archive, which is great. **luerzersarchive.net**

Creativity Online: Creativity Magazine in its print form had been around since 1986, but in 2009, they went all online. They have a huge archive of TV spots and a lot of print and online work too. Being online, it's very up to date on what's going on. The biggest problem with Creativity is that it's really expensive to subscribe, $99.95, and you have to subscribe to look at any work that's more than a week old. Usually art schools will have a subscription though. So if you end up at an art school (or have 100 bucks), you're golden. **creativity-online.com**

Communication Arts Magazine: This is a great, classic publication. They're best known in the advertising world for their yearly Advertising Annual (which I poured over endlessly as a student, and still do today). They also have award annuals for design, interactive and illustration. Their monthly editions are great too. True to its name, it features any kind of art that has a message, usually commercial, but not always. It has graphic design and advertising, print, TV, outdoor, online, and even some architecture and interior design. Good stuff. **commarts.com**

CMYK Magazine: This one should be of special interest to you as a student. It features only student work: advertising, graphic design, photography and fine arts. In other words, it's your competition and, as you'll discover from CMYK, your competition is freakin' talented. I'd highly recommend that you get a hold of a CMYK ASAP. Then you'll know right away the quality of work you need to produce. The site is a great resource too. You can check out student books and post your own. Highly recommended, and it's really affordable. **cmykmag.com**

Ads of The World: A decent online resource with tons of ads to look at. I find it pretty hit and miss (mostly miss), since it seems like they'll put up just about anything that gets sent to them, but it's definitely a good place to check out a massive amount of work for free. **adsoftheworld.com**

The FWA: Favourite Website Awards: Just what it sounds like. The FWA features the coolest sites going, mostly commercial sites, like microsites and online stuff promoting products, i.e. the kinds of stuff you're going to be tasked to come up with. This site will point you toward some of the most amazing, cutting edge online stuff out there. **thefwa.com**

Those will get you started. The major awards, The One Club (they put on the One Show), The Clios, The Andys (I'm serious, and it has nothing to do with me. I've never won one) and the Cannes Lions, just to name a few, have sites and award books you can track down too. The One Show Annual is especially great. It's expensive, but really good to look at. To avoid paying for it, often they'll have a copy or two of the One Show Annual at Barnes and Noble or other mega-chains like that, until they all close, anyway. Buy a coffee, pull up a chair and spend an hour or so going through it. No one is going to give you the "hey, this ain't a library" line at one of those big places.

There're also a series of books called, "Advertising Now," that I think are pretty good. They're easy to find online or at one of the big chain bookstores, and are surprisingly affordable for how thick they are.

Happy readin'.

PART IV:
GETTING SCHOOLED

THE QUESTION OF QUESTIONS WHEN IT COMES TO BUILDING YOUR BOOK: ART SCHOOL OR GO IT ALONE(ISH)?

*T*hroughout the book, I've hinted on the two main ways you can go about building your portfolio. One option is you can do it on your own. The other option is attending a school designed specifically to instruct you and guide you through the process, called **Art Schools** or **Portfolio Schools**. There's a little bit of difference between the two schools.

An art school usually has multiple programs, each focusing on helping students becoming better artists in different areas or vocations. Usually the artistry taught is of the commercial variety, like careers in graphic design, interior design, fashion design, film, illustration, photography, etc. Among their many programs, many art schools offer advertising portfolio development.

A couple good examples of these kinds of institutions are The Academy of Art University in San Francisco, California (which I've mentioned many times since I've got a history there) and Art Center in Pasadena, California.

Portfolio Schools, also known as **Ad Schools**, however, are pretty much totally focused on advertising portfolio development. The most well known ones are Miami Ad School (where I have also taught), which has campuses all over the place, Creative Circus, in Atlanta, Georgia and Portfolio Center, also in Atlanta. I'll give you a list of others at the end of this section. Every single one of the schools I've mentioned is a fantastic institution that has turned out more advertising super stars than you could shake a Clio at.

I won't beat around the bush on which route of portfolio development I recommend between doing it on your own or going to a school:

Go to school.

You may think this might be kinda weird coming from a guy who went it alone and successfully broke into the business. But, as an instructor, I'm also a guy who has spent a lot of time in art schools, and I'm telling you, between doing it solo and going to school, it's no competition.

When you go it alone, you toil away in a vacuum, getting whatever feedback you can scrounge up from contacts you make in the ad industry. If you go to school, you totally immerse yourself in a place full of like-minded individuals, taught by advertising professionals who have been hired to help you build a kick ass book. The art school experience is incredibly intense, super challenging and a great preview of life in an agency.

But I won't beat around the bush on another thing. Art schools are insanely expensive. Crazy expensive. Like, "Holy freakin' crap, that's expensive!" expensive. You're going to fall into one of two categories: You're family has dough and they may decide that paying for you to go to art school is something they can swing. If that's you, awesome, you're in a fortunate minority. If that's not you, welcome to the world of financial aid and student loans. If you've already graduated from a university, you may already be well acquainted with this world. I can't say exactly how much we're talking, because honestly, I don't know. But let's just say it's beyond the kind of money you're going to have in your piggy bank. Yes, coming up with the funds for art school is definitely a scary prospect. But the good news is that hundreds of thousands of students from all kinds of financial situations have pulled it off over the years, and there's no reason you can't too.

One thing that's actually cool (not sure if "cool" is the right word, but I'll go with it anyway) about the high cost of art school is that it really forces you to do your research, like reading this book! You really have to engage yourself in some soul searching as to whether you really want to be an ad creative. Because I'm here to tell you, the cost of art school is one of the easier-to-overcome obstacles you're going to face. Being a student at an art school is HARD. Filling out paperwork for a student loan is a piece of cake compared to pressing on and continuing to work your ass off when you—and the natural self-doubt that we humans tend to possess—have convinced yourself that it's highly likely that you're the least creative person on earth and that you'll never be able to produce a book good enough to get a job. An exaggeration? You'll see. *That*, friends, is an obstacle with a capital O, and one that the vast majority of you will face.

You don't go into that kind of battle unless you know victory is worth the wounds you will acquire. I digress, but I think that any digression that further alerts you to the difficulties you will face from time to time is an important one. But if you'll allow me one more digression: IT'S ALSO FUN! Seriously.

So what about that other option: doing it on your own? Well, it can be done. I'm living proof. But there's still no way I can recommend it over going to an art school, despite the fact that I pulled it off. For one, you need to play the odds. The better your book is, the better your odds of getting that first job. I look at the student book that got me my first job and, I swear, I don't know what Marlin Neufeld at JWT Tech saw in it. I guess he recognized some potential. Maybe it was a simpler time. Marlin was an old school guy. But I can say, without a doubt, I wouldn't have hired me. I would have done what Tyler Hampton, a pretty well-known copywriter, did when I showed him my student book: he looked up from my work and said, "You should go to art school."

If I had gone to art school, I would have definitely had a much better book and much better job opportunities. I have no regrets because I've had a nice little run in this business so far, and I fully plan on having that run get nicer as I get better at my job with more experience. But in my next life, I will go to art school.

All that being said, it can be done. There are plenty of clues in this book as to what kind of stuff you should have in your portfolio. Plus, the web is absolutely packed with inspiration in the form of other people's portfolios. I'm not saying plagiarize, obviously. But one of the big problems I ran into when I was putting together my book was that I didn't know what a good, "hirable" student book looked like. Successfully built portfolios just weren't available for me to check out and online portfolios just didn't exist. Hell, the web barely existed.

But this isn't the past, friends. It's the future! And what a glorious future it is! If you decide to go it alone, you've got an amazing resource at your fingertips. You *can* find examples of the work you're shooting for, quickly and easily. And I don't even need to tell you where to get it. JUST GOOGLE IT! Type in "advertising portfolios." Click. You're gonna find some stuff.

Another good way to find portfolios is on LinkedIn. Do a search for "copywriter" or "art director." A whoooooooole bunch of the fine folks who work in this industry will pop up. On most of those profiles you can find links to their portfolios under the Contact Info tab. If you take this approach, I would recommend you avoid senior people. You want to find people new to the business who still have a lot, if not all, student work. When you do a search, try throwing in the name of one of the ad schools I mentioned, like "copywriter miami ad school."

Also, I'll mention a couple books I know that may help you get your book together on your own. The one that's been around the longest is appropriately titled, "How to Get Your Book Together and Get a Job in Advertising" by Maxine Paetro. This book has been around for nearly three decades, but I know that Maxine tries to keep it up to date. Actually the latest edition that came out is called "How to Get Your Book Together and Get a Job in Advertising: 21st Century Edition." There's another one titled, "Pick Me: Breaking Into Advertising and Staying There" by Nancy Vonk. Are they good books? I don't know. I haven't read them. But they couldn't hurt. I know that's a pretty unhelpful answer, but I will say that if you're going to put your book together yourself, you should read them whether I've got an opinion on them or not, because you're going to need all the help you can get.

While we're on the subject of helpful books, another book I strongly recommend (this actually goes for art school students as well) is, "Hey Whipple, Squeeze This" by Luke Sullivan. This isn't really a how-to-build-a-portfolio book, but it's definitely written with the aspiring or junior ad creative in mind. Luke is a well-known, veteran copywriter/creative director and author of many pieces on the field of advertising. He's a highly entertaining writer. In fact, I'm totally trying to rip off Luke's loose style as I write this book (I believe that Luke also adds a lot of stuff to his writings for the sole purpose of entertaining himself with great results. My results? Well, I'm entertained!).

"Hey Whipple" gives a lot of great advice and has a don't-take-this-business-too-seriously attitude that is to be admired and emulated. And, as I said, it's entertaining, loose and fun, just like making ads should be. It's as close as you get to a classic book in the ad creative world. Pretty much every creative has read it. Add yourselves to that list.

A FEW MORE WORDS ABOUT WHAT HAPPENS AT A PORTFOLIO SCHOOL

I've made it pretty clear why I recommend art school over going it alone. But as this is a book of setting up expectations and revealing truths, I'll give you a run down on what goes on at said art schools.

Obviously, every school is going to do things a little differently, but I can give you a good idea of what to expect. I've taught at two of the biggies, as I've mentioned annoyingly often, and have known people who graduated from other art schools, so I can say with confidence that they all teach under the same workshop format. If you're not familiar with a workshop format, I'll give you the basics. You present your work to the class and an instructor and classmates (mostly the instructors, since they're the ones with the know-how and students tend to be shy with their opinions) let you know what they think. From this critiquing, you learn what works and what doesn't. One of the big reasons the workshop format is perfect for art schools is that it closely simulates the actual ad agency creative structure—the agency *experience,* if you will. Obviously, art school differs from agency life in many ways, but if you boil it down, they're the same: you're given assignments and you work your ass off to come up with campaign ideas, much like the hypothetical creative team I described in the earlier chapter. From there the bad ideas are thrown out, the so-so ones that have some potential are discussed in the hopes of making them better, and the good ones are also discussed in the hopes of making them even stronger. Then you work your ass off for another week (in multiple classes, by the way. Hey, I said it was a lot of work), and show the results to the class again for more critiquing and weeding out.

Eventually, you wade through the massive amount of crap you've come up with (just helping you start thickening your skin now) in the hopes of stumbling upon one really strong idea that you work on even further to turn into a pretty, polished, smart and awesome ad campaign that is worthy of your very own portfolio!

Then you do it again.

And you keep doing this.

Lather, get your work crapped on, repeat.

More accurately, come up with a ton of ideas, pick out the oh-so-rare great idea, make it pretty, repeat.

This is an over-simplification, of course, but essentially, that's what you do at art school. (You also make a bunch of new friends and party and make out with them in a new and exciting city, but I digress.) There are classes that concentrate a bit more on copywriting, some art direction. In some classes you'll concentrate on interactive campaigns. The goal is to give you a book that is not only kick ass, but well rounded.

The majority of campaigns you come up with won't go anywhere, and will die long before they reach your portfolio. Even more frustrating is when you do a ton of work to fully execute a campaign, but when it's all said and done, it doesn't merit getting into your portfolio. But you'll get used to it. It's going to happen a lot.

As intense as art school is, if you have the right attitude, as I've mentioned, it's actually a good time. And if it's not a good time, that's a problem, because you should be having fun creating ads with other motivated young people. No, it's not going to always be a picnic. You may even shed some tears while building your book. You'll definitely lose a lot of sleep. Let's face it: you essentially spend the majority of your time coming up with ideas that you know suck in search of that rare gem. But it's that pursuit that you should get off on.

Art school isn't just a good opportunity to learn to make ads, but also a good opportunity to figure out for sure if you actually *like* making ads. Do you dig the intensity? Do you handle the failure well? Do you take criticism in a smart and professional manner or like an overly defensive and sensitive little baby? Does it eat at you if your fellow students (future colleagues) are turning out better work than you? It should. Do you to turn it up a notch and work harder to make sure it doesn't happen again? All these questions will be important to ask yourself because how you handle art school will be similar to how you handle working at an agency. And if you discover that you're not feeling and enjoying the intensity, it's a good place to make attitude adjustments and *learn* to enjoy these things. It can be done.

ANY ART SCHOOL RECOMMENDATIONS, ANDY?

After I ramble a bit, you'll find a list of schools you can go to that will help you build a book. I wish I could say, "This one is the best" and give you some advice on which one is going to give you the best results, but I can't. Not because I'm a jerk, but because there's just no way to know. Most of these institutions hire ad professionals as instructors, so the instructor turnover tends to be very high. A result of this hiring method is that programs have their ups and downs as far as quality of instruction goes. Some of us ad pros make great instructors, but some really suck at it. So I can't really make a dead on recommendation. For the most part, things tend to even out. I'd just say factor in cost, geographic location and find comments by students. They won't be hard to find online. But take comments with a grain of salt. As you probably know, people tend to complain and bitch in online comment sections more than they compliment.

At the end of the day, how much you get out of art school is on you. So I'll make these art school recommendations that have nothing to do with the actual school you go to. Follow these and you can't go wrong, no matter which school you choose:

-Have fun and keep it loose, but learn to act like a self-starting, self-sufficient, and professional grown up from day one.

-Work your brain to the bone like the rest of your life depends on it because, if this is going to be your career, it sorta does. Also, the harder you work, the more fun you'll have, because kicking ass and creating great work is more fun than sucking, which is what you'll probably do if you slack.

-This is the grumpy instructor one: take responsibility for your work and your actions and don't make excuses. Unless you were attacked or something serious actually happened, no one gives a shit why you didn't get your work done. If I'm your instructor, I certainly don't. I'm not going to bust your balls for not getting your work done, and it's not because it's okay. It's not okay, but you already know that, so I'm not going to waste my time chasing you or giving you a lecture on the importance of hard work.

-Don't be a whiner. No one likes a whiner. Take it from a guy who has done his share of whining, and suddenly realized, "No one likes me." It's no fun.

-Almost without fail, if *everyone* thinks an idea of yours sucks except for you, it's probably because it sucks. Don't waste a bunch of time defending an idea no one likes. Move on.

-You will have instructors who give weak feedback and don't seem very into teaching the class. Deal with it and continue to work hard in the lame classes too. It's hard, but don't use a crappy instructor (or an instructor who is just exhausted or often absent because of they're crazy busy at their ad agency day job) as an excuse to slack off.

-Did I mention work hard?

AN INCOMPLETE LIST OF ART SCHOOLS:

The Creative Circus
Atlanta, Georgia
creativecircus.edu

Miami Ad School
Campuses in:
Miami, Florida; San Francisco, California; Minneapolis, Minnesota
Coming soon to Brooklyn, New York
Campuses also in Germany, Spain and Brazil.
miamiadschool.com

Art Center College of Design
Pasadena, California
artcenter.edu

Brainco
Minneapolis, Minnesota
They also offer some portfolio workshops in Austin, Dallas, Houston and San Antonio, Texas
braincomsa.com

Chicago Portfolio School
Chicago, Illinois
chicagoportfolio.com

Portfolio Center
Atlanta, Georgia
portfoliocenter.edu

Academy of Art University
San Francisco, California
academyart.edu

VCU Brandcenter
Richmond, Virginia
brandcenter.vcu.edu

Adhouse
New York, New York
adhousenyc.com

Austin Creative Department
Austin, Texas
austincreativedepartment.com

Houston School of Advertising
Houston, Texas
houstonschoolofadvertising.com

The Book Shop
Los Angeles area, California
thebookshopads.com

Another option to look into, especially if art schools are cost prohibitive, are local independent workshop courses taught by ad pros. They normally span about 10 sessions per course (as I think I stated in the intro, I've put on a few of these myself). There aren't a ton of these, unfortunately, but look around.

101 The Ad School
New York, New York
101theadschool.com

Milwaukee Portfolio School
Milwaukee, Wisconsin
mkeportfolioschool.com

As I said, this is probably an incomplete list. Jump on Google and I bet you'll find more. But this list includes all the most well known schools. And research the hell out of each of these. Each one is very different in how long the courses are, prices, admission requirements, degrees offered, etc. Shoot me a note if you think there's one that should be included in future editions. I'm not hard to find online.

PART VI:
SOME FINAL STUFF TO THINK ABOUT

AM I CUT OUT TO BE AN AD CREATIVE?

*T*errified yet?

Actually, I hope that all this info is getting you more excited than freaked out. You should be a little nervous and possibly feeling a tad overwhelmed and a little confused. But hopefully just a little, otherwise this book needs a re-write. But if you're also intrigued by the challenge, then that's a good sign. However, you may still be wondering if you're really cut out for working in the ad world.

This is a question that at one time, in my limited wisdom, I thought I'd be good at answering. At first I thought it was as simple as is this person creatively talented? Is this person a hard worker? If yes, then of course this person will be a successful ad creative. Right?

Wrong.

I was just looking at the obvious. *Obviously* you need to be a creative person. Do you need to be an extremely driven hard worker? Duh. I was kind of like one of those sportscasters who say things like, "If you don't play good defense, you're not going to win a lot of games." Brilliant insight there, genius.

However, after teaching hundreds of students, I've found that it's simply impossible to predict a person's chances of being a successful, happy, gainfully employed ad creative. In other words, we people are just too screwy and unpredictable for me, or anyone, to know what kind of person is going make a good ad creative.

Yes, there are glaring things, like if you're a math and science wiz who never really liked art class and flunked all your English classes, then advertising is probably not your best choice. If you're a wildly talented, daring artist, but your artistic endeavors usually center around your hatred of the capitalist, corporate machine, you may want to continue on your current path and stay out of a business that exists almost solely for the benefit of capitalism.

As an instructor who genuinely cares and wants his students to do well in the real world, the unpredictability of how my students are going to do is something I've had to learn to deal with. I've had students who just blew me away on a weekly basis with their raw talent, but after graduation didn't really have what it takes to hustle and do the things that it takes to get an agency job. Then I've had students who didn't have what I would call a huge talent, but they busted their asses and scraped and clawed hard for every great idea, and then had the same work ethic when it came to breaking into the ad world.

So, what I'm getting at is, I don't know how to tell you how to figure out if you're cut out to be an employed and happy ad creative. I could feed you a bunch of rhetorical crap, like we've all seen: Do you like drawing? Do you like writing? If you answered yes, then you may make a great advertising creative! Congratulations, Mr. Ad creator! Blah blah blah.

I could even attempt to get serious and pull together a bunch of questions that sound a lot more helpful, but truthfully, they wouldn't actually be any more helpful.

What I can do, however, is give you a few things to think about based on students I've had and, more importantly, co-workers I've had. Hopefully you can use them to decide for yourself if advertising is something you will enjoy. I want you to note the word "enjoy." There's a big difference between, "Can I get a job as an ad creative?" and "Will I find a career in advertising fulfilling and pretty fun?" Let's be idealistic and strive for a good life here, folks. Because if you don't enjoy the majority of your waking hours…why bother?

The deal is, the world of creating ads, when stripped down, is comprised of two pretty basic elements: creativity and capitalism. We ad creatives are artistic folks who find clever ways to sell stuff for our clients. You've got to be cool with both of those aspects: creativity *and* the fact that we're capitalist tools. Shills. Sales people, at least in an indirect way.

What I'm getting at is that you don't really need to figure out if you're creative. You already know that. Rather you need to figure out if you're okay with the fact that your art is being created to move product. Even more potentially problematic for some, you'll be dealing with people—people who write the checks that your employer uses to pay you—who are more concerned with the moving of said product than with your artistic vision.

As you can imagine, creativity and capitalism, or more specifically, creative people and people more concerned with moving product, is a potentially explosive concoction.

But I really want to qualify that last statement before we move on to dispel some myths about client side people. Yes, you will have your frustrations with clients. You won't always agree. And, yes, some aren't very smart. But what line of work doesn't have its share of dull tools? Agencies have them too. That's just life. But don't believe the lore that clients are just a bunch of suits with eyes only on the bottom line. That's a bad attitude to have and an inaccurate assumption. The majority of the clients I've worked with are really smart, and a lot of times really fun people who make some great calls creatively. Many of them are actually former ad agency people themselves. They want cool work just as much as you do, but they also have a responsibility to make sure your ads are a going to show a return on their investment, which when you think about it is absolutely reasonable.

I just wanted to get that in so you don't go into your first client meeting with a chip on your shoulder.

Back to what I was talking about.

I've often said, "I knew I'd make a great copywriter because I'm a poet with sales experience." And that's held true for me. If you're going to be a successful and, much, much more importantly, *happy* ad creative, you've got to be able to handle the fact that you work for The Man and are a part of the corporate machine. To take it one step further, you don't have to *love* the fact that you work for the man, but it helps if you at least like it.

Personally, I like it. I don't necessarily like what every company and corporation out there does to make money, but big picture, I dig capitalism. And of all the roles that must be played in capitalism, I think I've got one of the most enjoyable ones.

But that's big picture stuff. On a more day-to-day basis, you have to be cool with the fact that you're going to be interacting with business minded people quite a bit. Sometimes, those folks are going to have the power to make changes to your work, for better (yes, sometimes it is for the better) or for worse (yep, sometimes a lot worse).

Can you handle that truth?

Can you get over yourself and be a team player and be open to the fact that this guy with his khakis and his haircut may actually know what he's talking about? Or how about this terrifying scenario: maybe he actually *doesn't* know what he's talking about, and he makes your ad not nearly as cool as it was. Can you let it go and not turn into a whiny pain in everyone's butt?

Are you starting to see why these questions are a bit more important than, "Do you like to draw?" Creating ads is hardly the only thing you need to be a successful and, I'll say it again, because it's so very, very important, HAPPY ad creative.

You need to be diplomatic. You need to be tolerant. You need to *not* take yourself so seriously. Otherwise, being an ad creative is hard, miserable work.

I've worked with some people who are just incredibly bitter and miserable all the time. They let every little thing get them down and always play the victim. They hate these idiot clients that just don't understand their genius.

I'm not innocent of this behavior. Not at all. I've gone through bouts when *I* was that whiny little bitch. I'm sure there have been many conversations that took place behind my back about what a pain in the ass I was being. But I like to think that I've been able to snap out of it. I'm certainly much better at snapping out of it than I used to be. As I've matured (a relative term), I've realized that I'm getting paid pretty well to sit around with really cool, incredibly smart people and write little stories. I get to fly all over the place to make those stories into commercials. And those clients who may have pissed me off are making that possible. So realistically, I've got nothing to complain about. That's what I mean by getting over yourself.

And all this "be tolerant and diplomatic and get on with your life" stuff doesn't just apply to dealing with non-creative people. At times it can be very difficult to stay calm, cool and collected when you're dealing with other creatives. I've had times when I was very frustrated with my partner for not "getting" an idea I have. Then you've got your creative director. It's really tough when you bring a creative director an idea you love and they look at it, just kind of shrug and don't share your enthusiasm.

If you're the type of person that has a real hard time bouncing back from disappointment, I don't care how talented you are, you better steer clear of advertising because you're going to be unhappy at work and you're going to make those around you unhappy. And, given how many hours of our waking lives we spend at work, that's not a good thing.

Yeah, when it comes to the question, "Am I cut out to work in advertising?" whether you're creative enough is the easy part to figure out.

AM I CUT OUT TO BE AN AD CREATIVE? PART 2: MAKING ADS SOUNDS FUN, BUT AM I TOO OLD?

If you're a youngster, fresh out of high school or college, I'll let you off the hook. You can skip this section and go catch up on Facebook or go tweet, "reading this awesome book. u should check it out." But, then again, I think there'll be some inspiration for everyone. So, I take it back. Don't skip this section. But still do the tweet pimping my book.

I want to write this section because the ad creative world has the reputation for being a youngster's business. And for the most part, I can't dispute that. I got my first job at 27, and that's considered a little late. But during my time working in agencies and teaching in grad programs, I've come across some pretty cool people who've proved that even though the majority of people start their careers in their early to mid-twenties, you're not unwelcome if you're older.

The fact is there are a lot of people who just take a bit longer to figure out what they want to do, career-wise. And I'm here to say, what's the big deal?

We've got the rest of our lives to work, so if you're still figuring out what you want to do into your late 20s or early 30s, lucky you, you've still got *plenty* of years to work. Sure, it's not ideal, and if you're still bumping around into your mid 30s with no idea of what you want to do, it may be time to do some serious soul searching. But it's certainly not cause for the emotional self-abuse some people lay upon themselves for not having found a "real job" (A term I hate, especially since jobs traditionally considered "real" make people pretty miserable.) by the time they're 24. And, sheesh, it's certainly not a decision to be rushed.

Beyond dispelling the semi-myth that advertising is a young (wo)man's game, I'm writing this section because what I've found through teaching is that being an ad creative is one of those gigs that seems to be really attractive to second career people. By second career people I mean people who wake up one day and say something like, "Gee, being a (crappy job here) really isn't as cool as I thought it would be. Come to think of it, I'm totally miserable. And, given the fact that I think about jumping out of my office window more than just a couple times a day, maybe I should think about finding an alternative way to spend the majority of my time." But then they don't just say this. They act on it. It's very commendable. When most people just deal with their horrible jobs by bitching to co-workers, friends, and spouses, second career folks take a massive risk and do something about it. We're talking serious stones. I love love love my second career students. They ALWAYS work hard and never make excuses. Yep, that's my kind of student. And I'm not just talking about people who were in tedious office jobs or stuck in mid-management or a brutal sales job. I've had a child psychologist, high paid IT people, a CPA, and people in other respectable, high paying gigs that just didn't want to do it anymore. Obviously, by the time these people ended up in my classroom, they were no longer what would be considered "college age." Yet they all kicked ass, and because of the fact that these people had lived a little and already knew how to compose themselves like professionals, the ass kicking continued into agency life.

What I'm getting at is, no, you're no more "too old" to break into the ad biz than you would be into any other career.

In 2007, I had the honor of working alongside the creative team named Adweek Magazine's Most Promising New Creative Talent, Mike Brenner (copywriter) and Greg Coffin (art director). Mike had actually been a student of mine at The Academy of Art. The award was given to creatives that had made an impact on the industry, yet were rookies (I believe two years into their careers, or less). The reason that this is relevant is that when this extremely coveted award was bestowed upon them, Greg was 31 and Mike was 36. If Greg and Mike, had been scared off by the DOBs on their drivers licenses, Lee Clow and Alex Bogusky (google them, they're ad gods, and the name Bogusky has already been mentioned several times in this book) wouldn't have had the chance to cast their votes for Mike and Greg, winning them the award. Instead, some guys in their 20s would have won. And though they would have deserved it because all the nominees were awesome, the team with 67 years between them was better.

Another rad story I have is that of James Beal. He's a former student of mine, now working as a copywriter in San Francisco. James had already embarked on what is widely considered one of the most "professional" of professions. James was a lawyer. A freakin' lawyer!

As in, "This is my son. He's a lawyer."

"Ooooooh. Wonderful. You must be very proud."

Love 'em or hate 'em, being a lawyer is a respected gig with a fat paycheck and it takes a ton of work just to become a lawyer.

There's just one problem. For a lot of people, and I mean a lot, becoming a lawyer ends up being a tremendous mistake. They just don't dig it, and I've said many times, not digging your job is a problem. It certainly was for James. So he quit and enrolled at the Academy of Art and started building a portfolio. He graduated and landed a gig at a big agency. Miserable work life problem: solved. At least I hope so. I haven't talked to Mike in a bit.

So here's the deal on age: don't pay attention to it. Instead pay attention to your interests and general attitudes and figure out if they're in-line with being an ad creative. You need to love the media and love technology, especially all the social media stuff. There are some older people who are already in the ad world who have been around and have done incredible work, so they can get away with not being absolutely up to the second on everything that's going on in social media. But if you're just starting out in the business, you can't get away with that, so you need to be all over that stuff. But if you're in your 30s but still have the current pop culture and media knowledge of someone in their 20s, you're golden. And I don't mean that in a *Golden Girls* (Google it if you don't get the reference) or "golden years" way.

THE PSYCHOLOGY OF BUILDING A BOOK
or
HOW TO SUCK

I think I've pretty well exhausted the idea that although building a portfolio is a fun and creative process, it's also artistically very difficult and, as a result, is emotionally trying at times. The biggest reason for this is, as I mentioned early on, that while building your book you're going to spend the majority of your time failing. Falling flat on your face. Sucking. Being lame. Crapping the bed. Screwing the pooch. Wow! This is fun! Here, you try a few! I'll leave some space for some write-ins:

To start things off, let me tell you a little story.

When I was in college, I had a crazy, but ultimately extremely worthwhile summer job selling educational books, like homework guides, door-to-door. It was absolutely brutal and humbling (a much needed humbling, in my case), as you can imagine. I never had any doors slammed in my face or any other stereotypical door-to-door salesman abuse. Rude people were not what made the job hard. Most people were actually really polite. And even if they weren't it was no big deal. I laughed it off and was on to the next door. What made the job hard were those vast majority of times when I wasn't selling a damn thing. You know, failing. As one of my sales managers once said to us sales trainees, "Selling books is easy. What's hard is *not* selling books." Very profound.

How we deal with failure is probably the biggest key to succeeding. It's kind of a cliché, and there are probably a million lame inspirational posters based on the thought, but man, when it comes to building your portfolio, it doesn't get much more important.

I couldn't even pretend that I've the got the answer on how to best deal with the rough times. Not only am I not a psychologist, but I'm not always that great at it myself. It's hard. Also, everyone is different, so I'm not going to hand out generalized, "Hey you, turn that frown upside down" caliber advice. You need to do your very best to figure out for yourself what works for you.

I can, however, say that usually the best cure to periods of creative self-doubt is coming up with a great campaign idea. Nothing will make you feel better about your ability as a creative than creating something great. That's why when you're feeling your lowest and feel like quitting, you need to gut it out and just keep working. Unfortunately, great ideas don't create themselves while we drink, watch TV, mindlessly surf the web (my personal favorite), cry, or whatever it is you do personally while feeling sorry for yourself. It's easier said than done, but that's what you gotta do when you don't feel like working: work.

I don't want to give you the impression that I have to constantly talk students off a ledge, figuratively or literally, but I feel that counseling is part of my job when necessary. Maybe I'm making things sound more dramatic than they are, but one of the main purposes of this book is to eliminate as many future surprises as possible. It's not all gloom and doom, obviously. I just didn't think I needed to include a section on how to feel when you're doing well. We're all pretty good at being happy and excited. But how to be good at sucking? I thought that could use some going over.

And of course, like everything you do as a student, dealing with failure in school is great prep for when you get into the ad world. But it's going to be even tougher because obviously you're going to have the added pressure of people depending on you. And believe me, these people will be more than happy to let you know when you're work isn't up to snuff, which is double-hard because most like you're already putting massive pressure on yourself.

Just brace yourself for the inevitable low points, try not beat yourself up too much when they arrive and keep moving toward that next great campaign. It'll show up eventually, but only if you move toward it.

SIGNING OFF

Thanks so much for joining me. We've (well, I've) had a few laughs, and hopefully learned some stuff, too. I genuinely hope that I helped you come to some sort of a conclusion on whether you want to join my colleagues and me in the ad world. I think it's a good world. It's not always a blast, but you won't find any industry like it. It's an industry full of amazingly great and talented people (and a few assholes who are total hacks, but what are you gonna do about that?). If you're like me, from a pretty humble and modest background, you'll get to do things you imagined you'd get to do: travel to cool places, work with famous people, see your work on TV and eventually make some nice cash while you're at it. And I get to do all this stuff even though I'm by no means a hot shot in this industry. There are probably tons of people reading this who will one day totally smoke my career and get to do even more cool stuff. I sincerely hope you do. Good luck. And feel free to shoot me an email if you've got any questions. Oh, or if you find any typos or weird grammar stuff.

Happy creating,
Andy
eandybeach@gmail.com